THE PRIVACY HANDBOOK

Proven Countermeasures for Combating Threats to Privacy, Security, and Personal Freedom

MICHAEL CHESBRO

PALADIN PRESS • BOULDER, COLORADO

Also by Michael Chesbro:

The Complete Guide to E-Security: Using the Internet and E-Mail without Losing Your Privacy

Freeware Encryption and Security Programs: Protecting Your Computer and Your Privacy

Privacy for Sale: How Big Brother and Others Are Selling Your Private Secrets for Profit

Wilderness Evasion: A Guide to Hiding Out and Eluding Pursuit in Remote Areas

The Privacy Handbook: Proven Countermeasures for Combating Threats to Privacy, Security, and Personal Freedom
by Michael Chesbro

ISBN 1-58160-357-6
Printed in the United States of America

Published by Paladin Press, a division of
Paladin Enterprises, Inc.
Gunbarrel Tech Center
7077 Winchester Circle
Boulder, Colorado 80301 USA
+1.303.443.7250

Direct inquiries and/or orders to the above address.

Visit our Web site at www.paladin-press.com

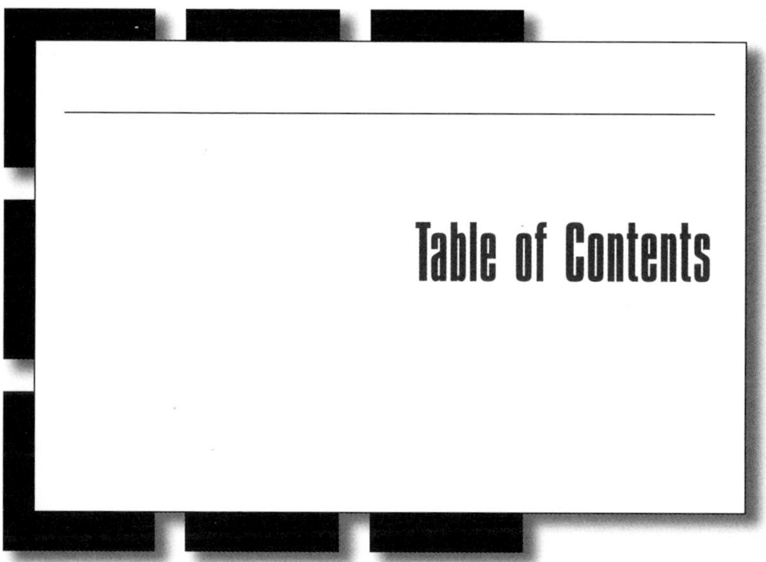

Table of Contents

PART I: COUNTERING THREATS TO FINANCIAL PRIVACY

PART II: COUNTERING THREATS TO COMPUTER AND ONLINE PRIVACY

PART III: COUNTERING THREATS TO PRIVATE COMMUNICATIONS

PART IV: COUNTERING THREATS TO HOME SECURITY AND PRIVACY

PART V: ENHANCING PRIVACY AND PERSONAL SECURITY: MISCELLANEOUS TIPS

PART VI: COUNTERING THREATS TO PERSONAL FREEDOM AND ACHIEVING SOVEREIGNTY

For

Joni, Skye, Tommi, and Max

Always and Forever

Preface

> *"Rightful Liberty is unobstructed action according to our will within limits drawn around us by the equal rights of others. I do not add 'within the law' because the law is often but the tyrant's will, and always so when it violates the rights of the individual."*
>
> —Thomas Jefferson

All of us want to feel that we are in control of our private lives. We all maintain an expectation of privacy in our homes. We assume that our telephone conversations are not being monitored and that our private mail isn't being read. We don't expect to be met with demands for "Photo ID" at every turn, and we assume that our private purchases are not being tracked and stored in some database for future reference. Unfortunately, this is not always the case.

There is a trend in government to want greater and greater control over "We the People," all in the name of providing better services and protecting us from harm. Businesses seek to develop profiles of their customers to improve direct marketing and advertising. Neighbors and family members may seek knowledge of our private affairs and seek to influence our decisions and conduct out of a true concern for our well-being, some personal need to get involved in our lives, or just unwelcome curiosity. Criminals seek information about us with specific intent to do us harm.

On September 11, 2001, the worst terrorist attacks in the history of these United States occurred on American soil, killing thousands of people, destroying the World Trade Center in New York, and causing significant damage to the Pentagon. These attacks were met with an outpouring of national unity, cooperation, faith, and patriotism on an impressive scale. At the same time there was a stream of proposals for numerous intrusions into the privacy, civil liberties, rights, and freedoms of American citizens, all in the name of preventing any such attack in the future.

These proposals for security at the expense of liberty were not made as part of some secret plan to undermine our rights and freedoms; rather, they were made by those in government who lack understanding of, or any concern for, the inalienable rights and freedoms that are the foundation of this great republic. These people propose to limit liberty in the name of safety, believing that some intrusion into our private lives is acceptable if it prevents future atrocity. Benjamin Franklin warned against this belief in 1759, stating, "Those who would give up essential liberty to purchase safety deserve neither liberty nor safety."

Unfortunately, there are those in government and the media who seem to believe otherwise. As the November 2001 issue of *America's First Freedom* magazine reported, "Following the terrorist attacks, former Secretary of State James Baker, former Secretary of Defense William Cohen, Tom Brokaw, and others said that Americans may have to accept 'some restrictions in civil liberties to guarantee security.'" It is a sad fact that no restriction on the liberties and freedoms of the American people is ever small, limited, or justifiable.

Case in point: on February 28, 1933, the evening after the Reichstag fire, the aging German President

Hindenburg was pressured by Chancellor Hitler into signing an emergency "Decree for the Protection of the People and the State," declaring:

> Restrictions on personal liberty, on the right of free expression of opinion, including freedom of the press; on the rights of assembly and association; and violations of the privacy of postal, telegraphic and telephonic communications and warrants for house searches, orders for confiscation as well as restrictions on property, are . . . permissible beyond the legal limits otherwise prescribed.

That which begins as a minor intrusion often becomes a major oppression with the passing of time. An example of this creeping plague on our liberties and freedoms is the ever-expanding use of Social Security numbers (SSNs). When the SSN was first proposed there was significant concern among the people that if we adopted such a system of assigning numbers to our citizens it would turn into a universal numbering and identification system. The government assured us that this would never happen. The SSN, we were promised, would only be used within the Social Security system, never as a means of identification or to cross-reference records and files about us. Initially, Social Security cards were even marked with the words "NOT FOR IDENTIFICATION." Today those promises and assurances from our government are exposed as being meaningless. SSNs are now used not only for Social Security purposes but also as taxpayer identification numbers and as required data to obtain a driver's or fishing license and just about any other type of government-issued license or permit. Social Security numbers are demanded when we want to open an account at a bank, apply for a credit card, or even rent a video from the local video store. As of October 1, 2000, federal law makes it mandatory that you disclose your SSN to obtain any type of government license or recreational permit. The law, 42 U.S.C. Section 666(a)(13), was enacted under the pretext of enforcing child support laws.

Many states strongly opposed the federal requirement for collection of Social Security numbers; however, the federal government simply threatened to withhold funding for support to the poor unless states complied with its onerous demand. As an example of federal extortion and abuse of our rightful liberty in this regard, we can look at the comments contained in Washington state law following the federal government's trampling underfoot of the people of that state:

> The legislature declares that enhancing the effectiveness of child support enforcement is an essential public policy goal, but that the use of social security numbers on licenses is an inappropriate, intrusive, and offensive method of improving enforceability. The legislature also finds that, in 1997, the federal government threatened sanction by withholding of funds for programs for poor families if states did not comply with a federal requirement to use social security numbers on licenses, thus causing the legislature to enact such provisions under protest. (Revised Code of Washington, Title 26, Chapter 23, Section 150)

Social Security numbers have become the universal identification number our government promised us would never happen!

But Social Security numbers are not the only infringement on our rights and freedoms. In the name of crime prevention, our right to keep and bear arms is hacked away at with this law, that regulation, and a string of proposals to do away with the Second Amendment to the Constitution of the United States of America. Similarly, in the name of preventing drunk drivers from hazarding our highways and byways, we run into police checkpoints where we are subjected to law enforcement scrutiny before being allowed to continue on our way. Fifty years ago, police checkpoints would have been protested as being a clearly unwarranted and unlawful search and detention. Today this trampling of our rightful liberty is tolerated by too many who subscribe to the misguided notion that it somehow makes us safer.

In the name of fighting the "war on drugs" and preventing terrorism, the government wants to have the ability to monitor all of our communications. This is already going on with systems like DCS1000 (formerly called "Carnivore"), even though such intrusions into the private communications of Americans are a clear violation of the Forth Amendment to the Constitution of the United States of America.

The September/October 2001 issue of *NMAF* (National Motorists Association Foundation) *News*, included an article about the Massachusetts Turnpike Authority (MTA) turning over "Fast Lane" records to criminal prosecutors. The Fast Lane system enables drivers to install a radio transponder in their vehicles to allow for the automatic billing of tolls in order to avoid having to stop at toll booths. The system records the date, time, and location of each charge, thus creating a record of the vehicle's location at a given time. The MTA repeatedly assured Fast Lane users that their customer account information would be held confidential and would not be used in any types of prosecution. However, as we see in the *NMFA News* article, these assurances were meaningless. This is just one more example of the government's pattern of lying to the people, breaking promises of confidentially on a whim, and collecting information for one purpose and then using it for another purpose entirely!

On October 26, 2001, President George W. Bush signed into law the USA Patriot Act. This is a broadly sweeping act putting restrictions on personal liberty, the right of free expression of opinion (including freedom of the press), and the rights of assembly and association; violating the privacy of postal, telegraphic, and telephonic communications; and facilitating the issuance of warrants for house searches, orders for confiscation, and restrictions on property.

The Electronic Frontier Foundation (www.eff.org) warned, "These are broad ranging, permanent reductions in civil liberties and privacy of all Americans. History has shown that such laws, passed in haste during a time of crisis, linger and cause difficulties long after the crisis has passed."

In his article "Will the War Kill the Bill of Rights?" Cato Institute adjunct scholar David Kopel warns, "Congress has passed terrorism bills granting vast powers to law enforcement that have nothing to do with counter-terrorism."

Charlotte Twight, a professor of economics at Boise State University, lawyer, and the author of *Dependent on D.C.: The Rise of Federal Control over the Lives of Ordinary Americans (*Palgrave/St. Martin's, January 2002), warns in her article "Watching You: Systematic Federal Surveillance of Ordinary Americans (*Independent Review: A Journal of Political Economy* Vol. 4 No. 2, Fall 1999, pp.165–200):

> Over the years, the federal government has instituted a variety of data collection programs that compel the production, retention, and dissemination of personal information about every American citizen.

> Linked through an individual's Social Security number, these labor, medical, education and financial databases now empower the federal government to obtain a detailed portrait of any person: the checks he writes, the types of causes he supports, and what he says "privately" to his doctor. Despite widespread public concern about preserving privacy, these data collection systems have been enacted in the name of "reducing fraud" and "promoting efficiency" in various government programs.

Does this mean that there is some secret conspiracy within the government to take away our rights and freedoms? Some long-standing organizations in the United States believe there is in fact a conspiracy within the government. The John Birch Society warns, "The threat to personal freedom and national independence is both imminent and immense—but not at all insurmountable." I don't personally believe there is an organized conspiracy or "shadow government." I do believe, however, that certain agencies and many officials within the government have lost all regard for our rights and freedoms and the principles upon which this great republic is founded.

One of the most blatant examples of this is the 1993 raid by the Bureau of Alcohol, Tobacco, and Firearms (BATF) on the Branch Davidian Church in Waco, Texas. The Branch Davidians are an offshoot of the Seventh Day Adventists and perhaps have completely different beliefs than you or I. It may even be argued that there was a need for government intervention into the activities of this church and its members. However, what an agency responsible for administration of a tax is doing conducting an armed raid on a church is a question that has yet to be answered. As we all know, the BATF raid on the church failed, resulting in a standoff between the government agents and the members of the church.

There is certainly a problem with machine gun-toting government agents conducting a raid on a church, but the real problem comes later as the government works to resolve the standoff. As those involved in the raid stated in testimony before Congress, the government planned to use heavy concentrations of tear gas to force the church members to come out and surrender. Now, these government agents knew that many of the Branch Davidians had gas masks to protect themselves from tear gas. These same agents also knew that there were several children in the church and that these children did not (and could not) have gas masks or any way to protect themselves from the effects of the gas. In the government's own words . . . the tear gas would cause the infants and children in the church to suffer from the effects of the gas, thus causing the parents to gather them up and come out and surrender. This is the ultimate example of a government totally out of control, with a complete disregard for the rights and freedoms of the people. Government agents, in a standoff with the parents of several innocent children, plan and then act to torture those children in order to force the parents to comply with government demands to surrender!

The raid on the church at Waco and the willful torture of infants and children by government agents are certainly among the most horrific atrocities committed against Americans, but the tragedy at Waco is certainly not an isolated incident.

It is an unfortunate fact that we must take precautions to protect ourselves against criminals, but we must also be watchful and protect ourselves against the unlawful acts of rogue government agents . . . Big Brother run amok!

Government intrusion into our private lives and infringement upon our rightful liberty are not the only threats we face. Identity theft, stalking, and criminal harassment are crimes that are on the rise and that directly affect our privacy and rightful liberties.

According to the Federal Trade Commission (FTC), between January 1, 2000, and December 31, 2000, there were 600,000 to 700,000 victims of identity theft in the United States. The FTC's own identity theft hotline received 40,000 calls from people who were victims of identity theft. Of the victims reporting this crime, 50 percent stated that someone had obtained credit cards and run up false charges using their identities, and 16 percent reported that fraudulent bank accounts had been established in their names. Telephone and utility services were obtained using the stolen identity in 25 percent of the cases reported. Of all of those reporting identity theft to the FTC hotline, more than half cited experiencing multiple problems as a result of the theft.

In addition to the crime of identity theft, another crime directly affecting our private lives is stalking. According to the National Center for the Victims of Crime (www.ncvc.org) 10 percent of Americans (8 percent of women and 2 percent of men) have been stalked at some point in their lifetime.

Stalkers do more than just sit outside your home at night or follow you around town. Stalkers pry into the most private affairs of their victims. They frequently have an obsession with their victim, seeking to gather the most personal details about the person's life. When we hear about stalking, we tend to think of people like Margaret Mary Ray, the woman who stalked David Letterman, or Robert John Bardo, who stalked and killed actress Rebecca Schaffer. However, the vast majority of stalking victims are just ordinary people, not celebrities or others in the public eye.

We may also tend to think of stalking in terms of men stalking women. However, this may not necessarily be the case. As stated in a National Institute of Justice (NIJ) research report entitled "Domestic Violence, Stalking, and Antistalking" (April 1996), "Stalking and domestic violence are gender-neutral crimes (stalkers and batterers can be either male or female)."

Anyone can become the intended victim of a stalker. However, the countermeasures used to protect yourself from other privacy-stealing criminals work equally well to protect you from stalkers.

Beyond the intrusions of government and the efforts of criminals outside of the government, some of us may face intrusions into our private affairs by friends or family members. On rare occasion the actions of these friends and family members are well meaning, unselfish, and taken completely out of love and legitimate concern. Most often, however, when friends or family members begin to intrude into your private affairs there is a self-serving motive behind their actions. Using terms such as, "for your own good," "tough love," and the like, they will sell your private property, look into your personal records and files, and try to get their hands on anything you may have of value . . . all the while demanding that you accept their actions as reasonable because they are "friends" or "family." Interestingly, the statistics about identity theft reveal that where the perpetrator of the crime was discovered, almost 12 percent of these criminals were family members, roommates, or other cohabitants.

In her book *Don't Shoot the Bastards (Yet)* (Loompanics Unlimited, May 1999), Claire Wolfe relates the story of Shirley Allen: In 1997 an Illinois judge, at the urging of Ms. Allen's family, ordered her to be taken into custody and committed to the state mental hospital for evaluation. Shirley Allen became a minor symbol of freedom and independence following her refusal to be taken from her home and incarcerated without warrant or trial . . . "for her own good." Ms. Allen held off Illinois police and government agents for 39 days until she was finally disabled and taken into custody. So . . . was Ms. Allen unable to care for herself, or was she a danger to the community? No, turns out she was just fine. She was simply an old woman who wanted to live her own life in her own way and be left alone. She did, however, own some property that her "loving" family discovered might not be coming their way anytime soon.

Finally, we come to corporate America. Businesses of every type gather information about their customers. Of course, there are times when a business needs information about a customer in order to complete the business at hand. (For instance, if you want a product delivered to your home, you will have to disclose your home address.) Too often, however, the reason businesses gather information about a customer has nothing to do with the transaction at hand. The businesses want your name, address, telephone number, and more for the purpose of marketing. They want to advertise new products, sales, and various deals. There is nothing wrong with a business developing a relationship with its customers. The problem comes about when these businesses take information you have provided to them as part of some business transaction and sell that information to other companies and organizations.

I believe that our personal information is just that—personal—and should not be used by others without our consent. This selling of personal information by unscrupulous businesses is such a blight on our right to privacy that we are seeing federal laws enacted, such as the Financial Services Modernization Act (Gramm-Leach-Bliley Act), which seek to give us the ability to safeguard our personal information.

So . . . what can We the People do to defend our rightful liberty? In answer, I offer a slight paraphrase of honorable men from our nation's past:

> We need only declare our independence, one by one, from the malignant culture that poisons our very lifeblood as a people. Our vision of a free and prosperous Nation continues the tradition of decentralization defended by virtuous and principled Patriots: Washington, Jefferson, Henry, Mason, Randolph, Calhoun, Davis and Lee. We daily accept expropriations from the central government, both material and spiritual, that would have brought these men to active resistance. They were willing to risk their lives, fortunes and sacred honor for the cause of liberty.

In this book I suggest several things we can do—short of armed revolution—to secure our personal privacy and individual freedom. Herein you will find techniques to protect yourself from the overly curious family member and the nosy neighbor. You will learn methods to protect yourself from criminals and to foil the intrusions of Big Brother into your private life. We will look at ways to keep unscrupulous businesses from invading your private life in the name of their profit. By employing the techniques herein, and by being aware of the threats we will discuss, you will improve the security and privacy of your life, while at the same time taking a stand in support of our rightful liberties.

INTRODUCTION

Threat and Vulnerability Awareness— The Onionskin Concept

Before we can take steps to protect ourselves from a threat, we have to be aware that the threat exists. Since you are reading a book about countering threats to your privacy, security, and rightful liberty, I assume that you are aware that threats exist—at least in a general sense. Throughout this book we will discuss various threats to our privacy, rights, and freedoms and look at some things we can do to protect ourselves from those who would invade our privacy, trample our rights, and strip away our freedoms.

Once we have identified a particular threat, we must ask ourselves whether we are vulnerable to that threat. For example, there is clearly a threat of having your e-mail monitored, but if you don't use e-mail or have an e-mail account, you have no vulnerability to that threat. There is a threat from stalkers or other criminals trying to steal your identity if they can obtain information about you from your trash, but if you use a paper shredder you have used a countermeasure to neutralize that threat.

As we identify potential threats to our privacy, security, and rightful liberty, we need to take steps to counter those threats. Unfortunately, there is no single thing that we can do to protect ourselves from all potential threats. Countermeasures are best employed in layers. This is sometimes called the "onionskin" concept, where several countermeasures or layers of security are in place, each wrapped around the other much like the skin of an onion, providing a protective covering for the onion itself.

The greatest threat to our privacy, freedom, and rightful liberty is the idea that there is no threat, that one has nothing to hide, and that even if there is some threat, there is nothing we can do about it. It is my hope that this book will dissuade you from this misguided notion.

Once we realize that there is in fact a clear and present danger facing us and are aware of the effect it can have on our freedom, we can start to do something about it.

So . . . let's start identifying threats to our privacy, freedom, and rightful liberty and building those layers of security to protect ourselves.

PART I

COUNTERING THREATS TO FINANCIAL PRIVACY

Chapter 1

Beware: Your Bank Is Spying on You!

Did you know that your bank is required to spy on you? The Bank Secrecy Act (31 U.S.C. 1051 et seq., 31 C.F.R. 103) requires your bank to maintain records of personal financial transactions that "have a high degree of usefulness in criminal, tax, and regulatory investigations and proceedings." It also requires that your bank report any "suspicious transaction relevant to a possible violation of law or regulation." These "Suspicious Transaction Reports" are sent to the Treasury Department's Financial Crimes Enforcement Network (FINCEN).

These reports are sent without your consent, and you are provided no notification that any such report has been filed about you. Once on file, these reports are available to more than 50 law enforcement agencies, including the FBI (the guys who provided the snipers at Ruby Ridge, Idaho, and Waco, Texas), U.S. Customs Service, and BATF, as well as every office of the U.S. Attorney. No court order is required for these agencies to obtain FINCEN reports about you. They need not show probable cause, reasonable suspicion, or even direct relevance to an ongoing investigation. Simply put, FINCEN reports are a pond where law enforcement agencies can conduct fishing expeditions looking for some possible irregularity in your banking transactions, which just might indicate that you may have committed some sort of crime.

This creates a serious problem that goes far beyond privacy concerns. In recent years law enforcement agencies have not been known for obtaining warrants that they then present after a knock on someone's door. Rather, these agencies tend to stage armed raids in the middle of the night, often with disastrous results, followed thereafter by elaborate cover-ups (Gordon Kahl, the Weavers at Ruby Ridge, the babies burned to death at the Church in Waco, Shirley Allen, Donald Scott, and many others).

But just what is your bank reporting to FINCEN? After all, you're no criminal trying to launder hundreds of thousands of ill-gotten dollars through your bank account. Well, your bank is reporting any combination of transactions totaling $5,000 or more, where the transaction

- involves funds derived from illegal activities
- is intended to conceal such funds to evade any law or regulation, including reporting regulations
- is designed to evade any Bank Secrecy Act regulation
- has no business or lawful purpose or is not the sort in which the particular customer would normally be expected to engage, and the financial institution has no reasonable explanation for the transaction after examining the available facts, including background and possible purpose of the transaction

Furthermore, your bank is required to report any transaction of $10,000 or more to the IRS regardless of its belief about the legality of the transaction itself.

Think about this for a minute. Your bank is required to report to FINCEN any transaction that "is not the sort in which the particular customer would normally be expected to engage." So, if your normal banking patterns indicate that you deposit your paycheck every week, write a few checks to pay your bills, and maybe take a couple hundred dollars in cash out of your savings account once in a while, what happens if you save up for a major purchase and take the money out all at once to make that purchase? What if you were to do some part-time work for a contractor and get paid upon completion of the project? It is not uncommon for contractors to do work preparing real estate for sale and to wait for payment until the sale goes through. Would a lump sum deposit from this work be one that "is not the sort in which the particular customer would normally be expected to engage?"

And while we're asking these questions, what right does your bank have to monitor and track your financial habits or to be in a position where it is able to report whether any particular transaction is the sort in which you would normally be expected to engage? Yes, I know, the Bank Secrecy Act gives it the right, but to me it seems just plain wrong!

If you agree that the Bank Secrecy Act allows an unwarranted invasion of your privacy and tends to trample your personal freedoms underfoot, beware, because worse is yet to come.

The following passage is from the *Federal Register* Vol. 63 No. 234, December 7, 1998, pp. 67515–67524:

> The Board of Governors of the Federal Reserve System (Board) is requesting comments on proposed regulations requiring domestic and foreign banking organizations supervised by the Board to develop and maintain ``Know Your Customer" pro-

> grams. As proposed, the regulations would require each banking organization to develop a program designed to determine the identity of its customers; determine its customers' sources of funds; determine, understand, and monitor the normal and expected transactions of its customers; and report appropriately any transactions of its customers that are determined to be suspicious, in accordance with the Board's existing suspicious activity reporting regulations.

The proposed regulations took up several pages of that issue of the *Register* in discussing how banks would be required to monitor our financial activity once the proposed regulation was adopted.

Fortunately, various groups brought the proposed "Know Your Customer" regulation to the attention of the general public. This resulted in a major outcry concerning this clearly unwarranted invasion of our privacy and complete disregard for our personal freedoms. As a result, the proposed regulation was withdrawn in March 1999. Even so, there is still one haunting sentence in the *Federal Register* concerning this oppressive regulation: "In many instances, monitoring is already occurring."

It was the massive public outcry that prevented the oppressive "Know Your Customer" proposal from becoming law, but this type of proposal is frequently being considered by government agencies and representatives who have no regard for our rightful liberty.

It is interesting to note, however, that even without such oppressive and intrusive rulings as the ill-conceived "Know Your Customer" regulation, Big Brother can already track every financial transaction you make . . . unless that transaction is made in cash. In the January 7, 2002, edition of *The Washington Post* were the following comments from Secretary of the Treasury Paul H. O'Neil: "One of the things that we were able to do after we identified all the people who were involved in the hijackings was to retrospectively create a spider web of all their financial connections. By having them identified, it made it possible *to go back and reconstruct every place that they touched the financial system.*" (Emphasis added.) Now in this case Secretary O'Neil was speaking of the on-going investigation into the September 11, 2001, terrorist attacks against the World Trade Center and the Pentagon, so the government was certainly applying all of its resources to this investigation. Even so, it is frightening to know that Big Brother can identify every place we touch the financial system when he chooses to do so.

Chapter 2

Establish a Foreign (Offshore) Bank Account

When you think of offshore banking you may think of major corporations seeking international position and advantage or the very rich looking to protect their assets. However, you don't have to be a major corporation or one of the world's 100 wealthiest men to want to protect your assets and maintain a degree of financial privacy.

It is an unfortunate fact that banks in the United States offer very little in the way of financial privacy to their customers. In fact, as we have seen, U.S. banks are actually required to spy on their customers, reporting their findings to the government. Furthermore, "asset forfeiture laws" (originally intended to fight international narcotics trafficking, now little more than theft in the name of the law) and IRS "Notices of Levy," which cause U.S. banks to seize your accounts without your ever being convicted of any crime in a court of law, are among the many possible reasons to look at offshore banking.

There is no real tradition of "banking privacy" in the United States. Because of this lack of financial privacy, it is often very easy for private investigators and various other snoops to obtain information about your U.S. bank accounts. The privacy of your accounts simply is not a high priority for most U.S. banks.

On the other hand, there is a very strong tradition of "banking privacy" among certain foreign banks. We have all heard about "secret Swiss bank accounts," but it is not just the Swiss that have very strict banking secrecy laws and a long tradition of protecting their clients' privacy interests. European banks in general tend to have a tradition of protecting their clients' privacy, and places like the Cayman Islands are also well known for their banking secrecy laws.

There is nothing illegal about an American citizen having an account in a foreign bank. Of course, you are supposed to voluntarily declare your income and pay any taxes you may lawfully owe to the United States, but this in no way prevents you from keeping your money overseas.

Once you have decided that an offshore bank account may be right for you, your next step will be to find a bank that can meet your needs. There are various groups that will help you establish an offshore bank account, and they will also charge you a fee of a few hundred to a couple thousand dollars for doing so. Fortunately, it is really not necessary to use these intermediaries and pay their associated fees, since many offshore banks have internal departments set up to assist foreigners in establishing accounts.

Contact various foreign banks directly and ask for information about the services they provide and their ability to meet your financial and privacy needs. The following are some things to consider:

- Minimum deposit (This may be as little as the equivalent of $100 to as high as $10,000.)
- Account maintenance and transaction fees (All banks have fees of one sort or another. Be sure to choose an offshore bank that offers you the lowest fees for the type of banking services you need.)
- Credit cards and ATMs (Most offshore banks will provide you with a secured credit card. You usually have to maintain a deposit of 125 percent of your credit limit. Once you have become an established client with the bank it may be possible to get an unsecured credit card—maybe!)
- Secure online transactions (Will you be able to access your accounts through a secure online connection—assuming you are not flying down to Grand Cayman every few weeks?)
- Association with U.S. banks (If you are establishing an offshore account to maintain financial privacy in the United States, be sure your chosen bank does not provide your account through a U.S. bank. For example, Mercury Bank (Grand Cayman) offers a U.S. dollar checking account, but these checks are processed through Nations Bank—a U.S. bank.)
- Taxes (You may be liable for taxes in the country where your offshore account is established. For example if you maintain a Swiss Franc account in a Swiss Bank, 35 percent of your interest is held for Swiss taxes. Be sure you establish an account that allows you to maintain a tax-exempt status.)
- Availability of funds (Your funds should be immediately available via credit, ATM, wire transfers, telephonic instruction to the bank, and so on. Sending a letter to your bank in Switzerland and waiting for a response by mail may not always be the best option for handling your accounts.)

There are a vast number of offshore banks that may meet your financial and privacy needs. Below are a few that are accustomed to dealing with foreign accounts and have a good reputation for efficiency and maintaining customer privacy.

Barclays Group
54 Lombard Street
London EC3P 3AH United Kingdom
www.barclays.com

Mercury Bank and Trust Ltd.
P.O. Box 2424
Caledonian House, 3rd Floor, Mary Street
George Town, Grand Cayman, Cayman Islands, BW.1
www.mercury.com.mx

Banque et Caisse d'Epargne de l'Etat, Luxembourg
P.O. Box 2105
L-1021 Luxembourg
www.bcee.lu

Liechtensteinische Landesbank Aktiengesellschaft
Postfach 9490
Vaduz Liechtenstein
www.llb.li

Credit Suisse
Postfach 1
8070 Zürich SKA
Switzerland
www.credit-suisse.com/en/home.html

One final note on offshore banking privacy—no bank is in the business of supporting criminals. If you are involved in international money laundering, narcotics trafficking, or some other serious crime, information about your accounts may be disclosed to officials of the country wherein you maintain your account (and possibly to officials in your country of residence). It is nice to note, however, that failure to pay U.S. taxes is not a crime in Switzerland, and a bank in Luxembourg has no interest in disclosing your past year's credit card purchases to a U.S. divorce court.

Because your purpose for offshore banking (and in fact the purpose of most individuals who establish offshore accounts) is financial security and personal privacy as opposed to criminal activity, you can take full advantage of many foreign countries' banking secrecy laws and longstanding tradition of protecting financial privacy.

Chapter 3

Use PayPal for Private Financial Transactions

PayPal (www.paypal.com) is an online payment service that allows you to send money to and receive money from any other person with a PayPal account. When you set up a PayPal account, it is associated with your bank account, credit card, or both. This allows you to send money to another PayPal account holder, having funds withdrawn from your bank account or charged to your credit card. It is also possible to maintain funds directly in your PayPal account online. These funds are accessed first before deducting money from your associated bank account or credit card. If you don't verify your PayPal account by associating it with a bank account or credit card, you are subject to a $1,000 spending limit.

OK, so PayPal may be a fast and convenient way of sending money online, but what does this have to do with security, you ask. The security advantage of PayPal is in the fact that it can serve as a hub for some of your financial transactions, preventing these transactions from being revealed in your bank or credit card records. Furthermore, when you pay someone with PayPal you don't disclose any of your personal financial information to that person, unlike when you write him a check or pay with your credit card.

When you access funds in your bank account or credit card through PayPal, the transaction is recorded on your bank statement as "PayPal E-Check" and on your credit card statement as "PayPal." Although this clearly reveals that you have a PayPal account, it does not identify the name of your PayPal account or where the money went after it was transferred through PayPal. Likewise, the person receiving a payment from you through PayPal has no idea what bank you use or any information about your account (such as checking account number and check number if you send a personal check, as well as your address, telephone number, or anything else you may have foolishly allowed to be printed on your checks).

Any competent investigator will be able to obtain information about your financial records by developing a source inside the bank, or through such things as pretext calls. However, by using PayPal as a hub between yourself and certain of your financial transactions, you make discovery of the details of your personal financial transactions that much more difficult. It adds one more layer to the onionskin of your personal security plan.

Regarding disclosure of your financial information, PayPal states the following:

> We will NEVER release an individual's personal information without consent. If you are a registered PayPal user, you have consented to have your name, email address, date of sign-up, and whether you have confirmed (or not confirmed) an account at another financial institution only made available

> to anyone whom you have paid or who is attempting to pay you through PayPal, as described in the Terms of Use. However, your credit card number, bank account and routing number, and other financial information will NEVER be revealed to anyone whom you have paid or who has paid you through PayPal. This makes PayPal transactions more private than mailing a check or giving out your credit card!

Now we must assume that PayPal would disclose details of your PayPal account pursuant to a subpoena or other legal process, but the intent of using PayPal as a security measure is not to enable you to conduct criminal activity but to add an extra degree of privacy to your financial transactions. When you sign up for a PayPal account it may also be worth the effort to send an e-mail to PayPal informing them of your interest in the privacy of your PayPal account and encouraging them to maintain and further enhance their privacy policies.

Chapter 4

Establish an E-Gold Account

E-gold (www.e-gold.com) is another online method of transferring money worldwide over the Internet. What makes e-gold unique is that it is 100-percent backed by gold (and other precious metals). This is an excellent concept.

There is no cost or obligation to establish an e-gold account. Once you have set up your account, of course, you need to make deposits to it. This can be done by transfer from other e-gold accounts. So if you have an online business or Web page, or perhaps you sell something using an online auction service (e.g., E-bay), you can accept e-gold payments. You may also fund your e-gold account by purchasing gold from an "independent exchange market maker" (e.g., London Gold Exchange) and having gold deposited to your account.

Another useful feature of e-gold is that it is possible to obtain an "offshore" credit/cash card associated with your e-gold account from places like Cash Cards International (www.cashcards.net). This lends a degree of privacy and anonymity to the use of your e-gold account.

Finally, if you have a private business you can accept e-gold as a form of payment and actually save money when compared to accepting the same payments using credit cards.

Chapter 5

Stop Financial Institutions from Selling Your Private Information

As part of their marketing strategy, your bank and other financial institutions may be selling your personally identifiable financial information. This information may be given to affiliates of the financial institution or sold to completely unrelated third parties, either companies or individuals. This is done without your permission, serving only to increase the profits of the bank at the expense of your privacy. If you receive a lot of "preapproved" credit offers (read junk mail), it is likely that the information used to obtain that preapproval was obtained from one of the financial institutions with which you now do business.

This complete disregard by various financial institutions for the privacy of its customers' personal information is so pervasive and offensive that the federal government passed the Financial Services Modernization Act

(Gramm-Leach-Bliley Act), allowing you to opt out of having your private financial data sold by your bank.

Some time prior to July 2001, you received a notice from your bank, credit card companies, and other financial institutions telling you that you had the right to prohibit them from selling your private financial information. This was very likely a notice included with your monthly statement and was in among the offer for a free pen set and notice of summer rates for new car loans . . . all the extra "stuffers" that many of us simply ignore.

After July 2001, if you did not "opt out" (that is, notify the financial institutions with which you do business that you did not want them to sell your private information to others), they were free to continue doing so. Thankfully, the Gramm-Leach-Bliley Act provides that you can opt out of your bank's marketing scheme at any time (even after July 2001). The following letter is an example of what you may want to send to your financial institutions to enhance your personal privacy and prevent your private financial data from being sold.

Date

Your Name
Your Address

Financial Institution Name (Bank, Credit Card, Credit Union, Investment, etc.)
Financial Institution Address

RE: Account Number(s) ______________________________

Dear Sir or Madam:

I am submitting the following instructions with regard to my account(s) and your information sharing and sales policies:

In accordance with the provisions of the Financial Services Modernization Act (Gramm-Leach-Bliley Act) allowing me to opt out of any sharing or sales of my personal information, I direct you not to share any of my personally identifiable information with nonaffiliated third-party companies or individuals. I further direct you not to share nonpublic personal information about me with affiliated companies or individuals.

In accordance with the Fair Credit Reporting Act, which allows me to opt out of the sharing of information about my creditworthiness, I direct you not to share such information with any affiliate of your company.

I do not wish to receive marketing offers from you or your affiliates. Please immediately remove my name from all marketing lists and databases. I request that you acknowledge receipt of these instructions and your intention to comply with my request for privacy of my personal, financial, and other information.

Thank you for your assistance in this matter and for taking steps to protect the privacy of your customers.

Sincerely,

Your Signature

Your Name

CHAPTER 6

Opt Out of Preapproved Credit Offers

Your credit reports are being screened without your knowledge or permission. The purpose of this screening is to market products and services to you through various mass mailings (junk mail)! If you have received offers for "preapproved" credit cards, loans, and accounts, it is likely that this preapproval was obtained by screening your credit reports.

You have the right to prohibit information contained in your credit report from being used in any transaction that is not initiated by you. You can protect your privacy and stem the flow of junk mail to your mailbox by opting out of these screenings. Call the automated opt-out number for the major credit reporting agencies (Experian, Equifax, Trans Union) 1-888-567-8688.

You will be asked to provide certain identifying information that will be used to exclude you from this screening for preapproved credit offers. Opting out of these preapproved offers does not limit your ability to apply for credit should you choose to do so; it simply restricts dissemination of your private financial data in cases where you did not initiate the transaction.

Chapter 7

Use Prepaid Credit Cards

Prepaid credit cards are excellent tools for enhancing personal privacy and security. A prepaid credit card contains the VISA or MasterCard logo and is accepted wherever VISA and MasterCard are accepted.

The difference between a prepaid credit card and a regular credit card or debit card is, as the name implies, that you purchase the prepaid card for a given amount and thereafter use it as you would any credit card. Because the card is "prepaid," you get no monthly bill and, unlike a debit card, it is not associated with a bank account. Prepaid credit cards are comparable to traveler's checks without the associated hassle of checks. Additionally, these prepaid credit cards allow you to make cash withdrawals from ATMs (up to the prepaid amount of the card).

There are various prepaid credit cards available, but the one I have found to be most useful is the AAA Everyday Funds VISA. The card can be obtained at any AAA office. You fill out basic information on a form to purchase the AAA Everyday Funds VISA at any AAA office and pay cash for the card. The information you'll be asked to provide when applying for the AAA Everyday Funds VISA may be more than is actually necessary, but you can pretty much put whatever information you want on the form. AAA doesn't check the information you provide.

In fact, I went to an AAA office and explained that I wanted to purchase an Everyday Funds VISA for a family member who would be traveling later in the month. I asked if I could provide his personal information for the card but have it sent to me so I could give it to him as a gift when he left for his trip. AAA had no problem with this whatsoever. AAA asks for the last four numbers of the SSN of the person who will be using the card but allows you to provide any four numbers if you object to this. The point here is that it takes little effort to obtain a prepaid credit card in almost any name you want. You will need an address where you can receive the card (it takes about 10 days), but that should be no problem.

Once you have the prepaid credit card in hand, you can add additional funds to the account at any AAA office and certain banks. This allows you to continue to use a card in a given name. You can also elect to use the card for a specific purchase or short period of time and then abandon it once you've used all of the funds you have loaded into the card.

The major advantage of the prepaid credit card is that it allows a degree of anonymity when shopping on the Internet, by telephone, or at other times where making a cash purchase is not a reasonable option. If using your prepaid credit card to place orders over the telephone, remember that all calls to 800 numbers identify the number from which the incoming call is being placed. Use a private courier (UPS, FedEx, etc.) for shipping, and have your order delivered to a commercial mail-receiving agency (CMRA), such as Mail Boxes Etc. or PostNet. Almost any of these CMRAs will receive a package for you from a private courier service on a one-time basis without requiring you to fill out any type of paperwork. Simply call the CMRA and ask if they will accept a package for you. Explain that you will be passing through town or visiting for a few days and need to receive something from UPS or FedEx. The CMRA will usually charge you $2 or $3 per package received, but there is no paperwork or ID requirement.

An additional advantage of the prepaid credit card is that it can be used to support alternate ID. Because credit cards are often accepted as a secondary form of ID, the prepaid credit card makes an excellent addition to any alternate identity one may be building. Perhaps you would like to travel under an assumed name. Using your prepaid credit card you can reserve a motel room, pay for various travel expenses, and more—and never have any of this associated with your name or appear as transactions in "your" financial records.

In addition to the AAA Everyday Funds VISA, there are several other prepaid credit cards available that may meet your individual needs. Following are some possibilities:

- AAA Everyday Funds VISA (www.storedvalue.aaa.com)
- CashX (www.cashx.com)
- E-Count MasterCard (www.ecount.com)
- NetSpend (www.netspend.com)
- VISABuxx (www.visabuxx.com)

Some of the prepaid cards (i.e., E-Count and VISABuxx) require that the card be associated with an existing account. Others allow direct purchase of the card and are not associated with any other type of account

(AAA Everyday Funds, CashX, and NetSpend). From a privacy standpoint, prepaid credit cards that are not associated with any other type of account are the best option, but cards linked to some other account may also be useful in certain circumstances.

I strongly recommend that before you get any type of prepaid credit card, you review the terms and conditions of more than one provider and then choose the one that best meets your personal privacy needs.

Chapter 8

Refuse to Show ID for Credit Card Transactions

Recently some unscrupulous merchants have begun demanding photo ID from customers as a condition of using a credit card to make a purchase. This violates the privacy policies of both VISA and MasterCard!

These same merchants will tell you that VISA and MasterCard require them to demand photo ID before accepting your credit card. THIS IS A LIE! Neither VISA nor MasterCard require you to present additional ID or other supplementary information if your credit card is properly signed when presented to the merchant. In fact, they actually prohibit merchants from requesting additional identification as a condition of your using a credit card to pay for your purchase.

Regarding a demand for photo ID, VISA says,

> Please be assured that merchants may not refuse to honor a Visa card simply because a cardholder refuses a request for supplementary information.

> The only exception is when a Visa card is unsigned when presented. In this situation, a merchant must obtain authorization, review additional identification, and require the cardholder to sign the card before completing a transaction.
>
> —VISA International, Owings Mills, MD

MasterCard says,

> The merchant cannot require additional identification as a standard business practice when you use MasterCard for payment. There are a few exceptions, such as when additional information is required to complete the transaction. For example, a merchant will need your address if goods are to be delivered to your home.
>
> —MasterCard International, St. Louis, MO

MasterCard is so concerned about protecting its cardholders from unscrupulous merchants and their improper demands for ID that it has established a special toll-free number for reporting this oppressive conduct. Call MasterCard at 1-800-300-3069.

So the next time some jackbooted thug demands your "photo ID" while you're shopping, let him or her know that such demands went out with the Nazis. Report all such abusive demands, and TAKE YOUR BUSINESS ELSEWHERE! Let's put the ID Nazis out of business!

Chapter 9

Limit Your Use of Personal Checks and the Information on Them

Most people who have a job end up with a checking account at their local bank or credit union sooner or later. Checks give you convenient access to funds you have on deposit with your financial institution. They also provide a permanent record of your financial transactions. Remember, your bank or credit union makes a copy of all of your processed checks. Checks also provide significant information about you to any person to whom you write a check.

When most people order checks they have a significant amount of additional information printed on them—information that is not necessary. Look at your own personal checks. You probably have your name, address, and telephone number printed on them. Some people will also have their SSN and/or driver's license number printed on their checks. This gives anyone to whom you write a check (or who happens to see one of your checks and is able to record the information on it) enough information to gain access to your account.

Many retailers accept personal checks as a convenience to their customers but will almost always demand significant personal data to be recorded on the check before accepting it (which is why many people will have this type of information preprinted on their checks in the first place). This is the retailer's right, since there is nothing requiring him to accept checks. By accepting personal checks, the retailer takes certain risks. If there are not sufficient funds in your account and the bank refuses to honor your check, the retailer is out the amount of the check. The information he asks for and records on your check gives him someplace to start tracking you down to demand payment if your check is no good.

To support merchants who accept personal checks, many banks have set up automated funds availability verification systems. This allows merchants (or anyone else) accepting a check to call the bank from a touch-tone telephone and verify that funds are available to cover the amount of a check presented for a purchase or payment. The way this works is that the merchant calls the bank and gets an automated response from the check verification system. He will be asked to enter the checking account number (printed on the check) and the amount of the check in question. The verification system matches the checking account number and requested amount against bank records and will then state either that funds are currently available or that funds are not available (often stated as "we are unable to verify fund availability at this time"). Now, this is a fine service for merchants, but it also allows anyone with the information from one of your checks to determine how much money you have in your account.

To determine the amount of money in your account, I can simply use the funds availability verification system and ask it to confirm availability of funds for a $500 check. If funds are available, I call back and ask it to verify $1,000. If funds are not available, I call back and ask it to verify $750. Once I have a bracketed range of funds available and funds not available, I simply call the system a half-dozen more times, bringing the requested amount closer and closer to the "not available" amount. I then know the balance of your account within several dollars.

Because the check verification system for many banks is an automated affair, I can get away with making several inquiries about your account with no one ever being aware that these inquiries were made. Check verification is usually not logged by these systems, and even if it is, it does not appear on your monthly statement so you will remain unaware that I have been examining your account.

I advise against ever presenting a check in person for any type of purchase. If you use checks, they should only be used for payment of routine bills by mail. Never write checks to pay for purchases in person, and be aware of what purchases you make by check through the mail. Remember that the transaction will become a permanent part of your banking records.

The only additional information you should have printed on your checks is your name! No address, telephone, and absolutely no SSN or driver's license number. This is never a problem when using checks to pay established accounts (electric bill, phone bill, etc.). Utility companies will process your check along with every other payment, and if your check bounces they just turn off your service. If you include a check as payment for some item you order through the mail, it doesn't matter if you have limited information printed on the check itself. Your order will be processed from the order form, not the check. The business will either ship your order immediately or, as a matter of policy, delay shipment until your check clears the bank. If the business has a policy of holding shipments until personal checks clear, it doesn't matter how much personal information you have printed on the check (or the lack thereof); your order will still be held until the check clears.

By using checks only for routine payment of established accounts and certain purchases by mail, you eliminate any need to have your "life history" printed on the face of your checks. However, for those of you who feel the need to use checking accounts for in-person purchases, I recommend that you obtain a debit card (check card) from your bank and use that in place of paper checks. Most retailers that will accept a personal check are also set up to accept credit and debit cards. Since most of these cards also contain the MasterCard or VISA logo, they should not require any type of ID to be presented for their use. (See Chapter 8: Refuse to Show ID for Credit Card Transactions.) You will be required to enter a personal identification number (PIN) on a keypad, which confirms your identity as far as the merchant and bank are concerned.

Personal checks have their place, but it is important to remember that there are certain privacy risks associated with using checks. By understanding these risks you can make informed decisions as to when writing a personal check will be OK and when another form of payment would be more appropriate.

Chapter 10

Attach a Telephone Password to Your Accounts

Your bank, credit card companies, investments, utilities, and most other places where you maintain some type of account will all generally accept telephonic inquiries about the account and conduct certain actions based on instructions given over the telephone. They do this for the convenience of their customers, and it's a service that most of us take advantage of, at least once in a while.

The problem with telephonic inquiries and instructions is that the customer service rep on the receiving end of the call has no real way to know whether the caller is actually the account holder or not. Of course, you will have to provide your name, and possibly an account number (although, if you claim not to have your account number handy most businesses will look up your account by name). Now, most businesses will ask for additional identifying information, but this is almost always limited to three pieces of information: your date of birth, your mother's maiden name, and your SSN. All three of these pieces of information are easy to discover about any individual. Your date of birth and mother's maiden name are available from public records (your birth certificate), and your SSN is so readily available as to make it useless as a means of authenticating someone's identity over the telephone. In fact, use of the SSN poses such a great danger of fraud and identity theft that any business using it for identification or authentication purposes is acting irresponsibly.

Social engineering, telephone scams, pretext calls, and ruses all come down to the same thing—someone getting information he is not supposed to have by tricking the person on the other end of the line into revealing it. The famous (infamous) hacker Kevin Mitnick has said that he was so often able to obtain passwords and private data by making a couple of telephone calls and having a convincing story that he seldom needed to resort to technical skills to hack into a computer system.

To protect your personal accounts from this type of social engineering, you should establish a password that is required in addition to any other "identifying" or "authenticating" information before a business will provide any type of information or take any type of action regarding your account based on a telephone call. Most quality businesses already have a procedure in place for individuals to establish passwords on their accounts. Even those businesses that don't have a specific procedure in place for account passwords can usually accommodate a customer wanting to establish a little extra security and privacy for his account. If not, consider taking your business elsewhere. Any business that won't take steps to protect the confidentiality of your account information should not be trusted with your business.

The password you establish can be almost anything but should probably be just one or two words that can be given over the telephone. Once you have established a password to protect your accounts, verify that it is being used. When you call a business to make an inquiry about your account, be sure that they ask for and receive the correct password before disclosing any information about your account. If you ever call and are not asked for your password or are provided with information about your account without giving the correct password, it is time to raise hell! Get the name of the person who disclosed your private information without proper authority and complain in writing to the general manager of the company. The security of your private information and a business' fiduciary duty to safeguard that information should not be taken lightly.

Even if you never make telephonic inquiries about your accounts, it is still worthwhile to establish a password to prevent someone else from doing so. Remember, every security precaution you put in place is one more reason for a criminal to go target someone else!

Part II

COUNTERING THREATS TO COMPUTER AND ONLINE SECURITY

Chapter 11

Safeguard Your Computer Files

In his book *Incident Response*, Kevin Mandia, director of computer forensics at Foundstone, states:

> Computers harbor more personal information and secrets than anyone can discard into a 20-gallon trash container. A typical computer holds information people once stored in wallets, cameras, contact lists, calendars, and filing cabinets. Computers are the treasure trove of personal contacts, personal finance, and correspondence. Practically every investigation—from simple theft to corporate espionage—can benefit from the proper analysis of the suspect's computer systems.

I quote Mandia here because his job as a computer forensics specialist is to acquire data from computers in the possession of suspects in various types of investigations. I fully agree with his assessment and want to further stress the importance of safeguarding your computer files. If you are like most people, your computer contains extensive personal information that you probably don't want disclosed to the public.

Think about what is on your computer . . . copies of e-mail sent and received; your budget and other information about your personal finances; your address book; digital photographs of your family, your friends, and yourself; your private diary. All of this and potentially much more is available to anyone gaining access to your computer.

One of the most effective ways of safeguarding information stored on your computer is to encrypt those files. In my book *Freeware Encryption and Security Programs* (Paladin Press, 2001), I discuss several free programs that will allow you to secure files on your computer. One of these is ScramDisk, which, although it was recently replaced by an updated version called DriveCrypt, is still available online at www.scramdisk.clara.net. ScramDisk is freeware, and it is one of the programs I strongly recommend to people who want to secure their personal computer.

Chapter 12

Use Passwords to Protect MS Word and Excel 97/2000 Documents

For those of you using Microsoft Word and Excel (as well as other MS Office products), you can add a password to your documents to prevent their being opened or modified.

I am not particularly a fan of Microsoft password protection schemes; however, there have been some improvements to MS Word and Excel 97/2000 in the algorithm used to protect documents from being opened. Comments from two companies specializing in password recovery, Elcomsoft and Access Data, indicate that a properly constructed password used with MS Word and Excel 97/2000 makes unauthorized access to the document difficult and time-consuming.

ELCOMSOFT

When you assign the "open" password to your Word or Excel 97/2000 document (so the user will have to enter it to open the file), Microsoft Office encrypts the document using relatively complicated algorithm (without storing the password itself inside the file), so it is impossible to retrieve it at all. However, AO2000PR can recover the lost password using the brute-force and dictionary attacks.

ACCESS DATA

Most Office 97 & 2000 recoveries take substantially longer than recoveries for other programs. Recovery times vary, but most Office 97 & 2000 recoveries will take about a day per character in the password. The success rate varies with Office 97 & 2000 and recovers about 80–85 percent of the passwords. Password recovery is not 100-percent guaranteed because the attack involves trying to guess what the password would be by cycling through a word list (list of potential passwords). If your password cannot be created from the word list, the recovery will fail. For Office 97 & 2000 recoveries, we recommend that you use one of our dictionaries.

To assign a password to your MS Word or Excel documents,

1. Open the document.
2. On the File menu, click Save As.
3. Click Options.
4. In the "password to open" box, type a password and then click OK.
5. In the "reenter password to open" box, type the password again and then click OK.
6. Click Save.

For Microsoft Word and Excel 97/2000 this offers a moderate degree of protection, if and only if you have a properly constructed password. A short password (4 characters) is recoverable in just a couple of minutes using a brute-force attack, and longer passwords can be recovered quickly using a dictionary attack if your password is an actual word. (Of course this applies to any password scheme, regardless of the strength of the algorithm.) The increased algorithm strength is only applicable to MS Word and Excel 97/2000 and does not apply to other Microsoft products and older versions of Word and Excel.

It should be clearly understood that the Microsoft password scheme does *not* provide a high degree of security. However, if you have nothing else, the password functions of MS Word and Excel can offer some degree of security. This will not stop a determined technical attack, but it will certainly slow down the casual snoop.

Chapter 13

Install a BIOS Password on All Your Computers

Who's accessing your computer when you're not around? Do you have a computer at work that is accessible to coworkers, the cleaning staff, or others? Is your roommate, a snoopy family member, or someone else playing with your computer or browsing through your personal files when you are not home? Even if you have a password on some files, it may be possible to get around that password by booting the computer from a floppy disk and accessing the files from DOS. There is, however, a way to stop all but the most determined from gaining access to your computer files. That way is with a BIOS password.

When you turn on your computer, certain things happen before you are able to access information stored on the system or run any programs. One of the first things the computer does during startup is to access the BIOS, or basic input-output system. This is information stored on a chip that tells the computer how to operate and where to access information on the system. If the computer does not obtain information from the BIOS, the computer will not boot and the startup functions are halted.

As a security function, you can add a password to the BIOS, causing the computer to stop and wait for specific input from the keyboard before completing the startup (boot) functions. To access the BIOS, you will have to perform certain actions during the startup functions of the computer. Normally you will see an instruction on the screen that says something like "Press F1 To Enter Setup." Access to the BIOS is not always obtained by pressing F1. It depends on your system, and any key or set of keystrokes may be required (e.g., on the Compaq Presario you press F10). You'll normally have a couple of seconds to access the BIOS before the startup process proceeds.

Once you have accessed the BIOS, you will see several options, which vary somewhat from computer to computer. You should see an option of establishing a password somewhere on the setup screens. There will often be two password settings available—one for accessing the BIOS (which you have just done) and the other to start the computer (sometimes called a power-on password). The password you want to set is the "power on" or "startup" password. Choose your password carefully and enter it into the BIOS password field. Be absolutely sure that you remember your password. You will not be able to access your computer without it. Now save your new settings and exit the BIOS. Your computer will probably reboot and should halt at the beginning of the process and ask you for the password that you just set.

Because a BIOS password stops the computer before it accesses any drives or information stored on the system itself, standard password-cracking programs will be ineffective. You will not, for example, be able to boot the computer from a floppy disk to get around the password, as is sometimes the case with a password function stored on the hard-drive of the computer.

If you forget your BIOS password, it is possible to access the information on your system, but you will have to disassemble your computer to do it. One option is to remove the hard-drive from the computer and install it in a computer that does not have a BIOS password. This does not change the BIOS password on your first system but is a method of accessing data on a system with a BIOS password.

It is also possible to clear the password function from the BIOS by removing all power to the system. This means much more than just unplugging your computer. All computers have a battery that provides power to such things as the BIOS when the computer is unplugged. These batteries may be soldered onto the motherboard or located elsewhere with a jumper providing the necessary connection. If you remove this battery (and the computer is unplugged), you have removed all power from the system, which should clear the password from the BIOS. Thereafter, you should be able to replace the battery, reassemble your computer, and start the system without being asked for the BIOS password.

The advantage to setting a BIOS password on your computer is that it stops anyone trying to access your system dead in his tracks unless he knows the password or is prepared to disassemble your computer to bypass it.

Chapter 14

Set a Desktop Icon to Activate Your Screen Saver

The password function associated with the MS Windows screen saver application does not provide a great deal of security and, to be fair, it's not intended to do so. The purpose of the screen saver is to blank your computer screen (or run some type of animation) after a set period of inactivity. The password function associated with the screen saver stops someone from being able to access your computer simply by pressing a key or moving the mouse, thereby turning off the screen saver. This is useful if you leave your computer unattended for a few minutes, providing low-level security while you are away from your desk. The problem is that most people set their screen savers to activate after 10 to 15 minutes of no activity. This leaves your computer accessible for 10 to 15 minutes each time you step away from your desk.

It is a simple matter to create a shortcut to your chosen screen saver and place that icon on your Windows Desktop. That way, if you have to step away from your desk for a short time, simply click on the screen saver icon.

Your screen savers are usually found in C:\Windows\System . . . on your computer. You can find all of the screen savers on your computer by using the Find Files or Folders function from the Windows Start menu and searching for "*.scr" (no quotation marks).

You should now create a shortcut to the screen saver file you have set to run after a set period of time and for which you have set up a screen saver password. If you don't know how to create a shortcut on your desktop, instructions are in the Windows Help file, which says:

To put a shortcut on the desktop

*In **My Computer** or Windows Explorer, click the item, such as a file, program, folder, printer, or computer, for which you want to create a shortcut.*

*On the **File** menu, click **Create Shortcut**.*

Drag the shortcut icon onto the desktop.

Now, just make it a habit to click on the screen saver shortcut anytime you are going to be away from your computer for a few minutes. The screen saver will activate and the password function will offer some degree of protection for your system while you are gone. Of course, if you are going to be gone for more than a few minutes you should shut down your computer so that it must be restarted and requires a BIOS password to start up again.

CHAPTER 15

Store Multiple Passwords Safely

The primary means of authenticating your identity online is through the use of a password or passphrase. A properly constructed password such as *ah83:B8soKv!Io9* provides reasonable security, but because many people find such passwords difficult to remember, they tend to use short, simple one-word passwords. Even if someone does remember a properly constructed, strong password, there are many different sites and accounts that require a password, so the same password tends to be used for all accounts. All too common is the worst-case scenario, where someone uses a simple password for multiple accounts. When this weak password is compromised on one account, all other accounts used by this individual are compromised.

Think about your own use of passwords. Do you use a password that is less than eight characters? Is it a word found in a dictionary? Do you use it on more than one account? If you were able to answer no to each of these questions, you are one of a rare few, or you already use a password safe.

A password safe is a means of storing all your passwords in a single, secured location. It is a small computer program wherein you list your accounts and passwords. The password safe secures these passwords by some type of encryption, allowing you to access them only after you have accessed the password safe (usually by its own password). Now you have to remember only a single password—the one that unlocks the safe.

After accessing your password safe, you can usually just select the account name you want to access and have your password for that account pasted to the appropriate area. Because there is no need to remember multiple passwords, you can create long, complicated passwords and choose a separate password for each account. Stronger passwords mean stronger security for accounts protected by a password.

One of the better password safes was created by leading Internet security expert Bruce Schneier, cofounder of Counterpane Internet Security, Inc. and creator of the Blowfish and Twofish encryption algorithms. His password safe is available as freeware on the Counterpane Web site at www.counterpane.com/labs.html. Bruce Schneier's password safe secures your passwords with extremely strong encryption yet is simple to use.

In addition to securing online passwords, the password safe can also be used to store credit card numbers, private telephone numbers, encryption/decryption keys, and similar information.

Chapter 16

Defend against Keystroke Monitoring

One of the greatest dangers to privacy of your electronically stored files and online communications is keystroke monitoring. A keystroke-monitoring program simply records everything you type on your keyboard and everything you click on with your computer's mouse, storing this information in a hidden file on your computer. Some of the more advanced keystroke monitoring programs will send the file with your recorded keystrokes to a designated e-mail address the next time you connect to the Internet.

One company, SpectorSoft (www.spectorsoft.com), advertises its keystroke monitoring programs saying, "Automatically record everything your spouse, children, and employees do online." I have seen these programs in use, and they do just what they say they will do . . . record everything you do on your computer! These programs are available to anyone willing to pay the price (around $100) and are easy to set up and run. There are even various shareware/freeware keystroke-monitoring programs available on the Internet that will give you this monitoring capability.

Once a keystroke-monitoring program has been installed on your computer, it can be very difficult to detect. These programs are, after all, designed to remain hidden and surreptitiously record your computer activity. The best defense against keystroke monitoring is to prevent the program from being installed in the first place. Preventing physical access to your computer and using techniques such as BIOS passwords to restrict unauthorized operation of your computer can keep unauthorized programs from being installed. Internet security programs by companies like Norton and McAfee can warn you of programs attempting to send designated information to the Internet. You should also make it a point to be aware of what is on your computer. What do the Autoexec.bat and Config.sys files look like? What programs are in your Startup folder and your Programs folder? Now you may not want to become a "computer expert," but it certainly pays to be an informed user.

Even if you are able to prevent someone from installing a keystroke-monitoring program on your computer, there is still a way to monitor your computer activity! Keystroke monitoring can be accomplished by attaching an external monitoring device to your computer. One such device is "KeyKatch," a small device (2.15 inches long x .635 inch in diameter, or about the size of the plug on your computer keyboard cable) that connects between your keyboard and your CPU. Simply plug the KeyKatch device into the back of the computer you want to monitor and then plug the keyboard for that computer into KeyKatch. KeyKatch will then record the next 8,000 to 64,000 keystrokes (depending on which model of KeyKatch you have). This information is stored in the

KeyKatch device, which can be removed from the monitored computer and downloaded at your convenience.

KeyKatch advertising states, "The **KeyKatch™** is a tiny recording device that attaches to your keyboard cable. It records all keystrokes typed on the computer. It doesn't require any external power source and it installs in seconds!"

I have used KeyKatch, and it does exactly what it says it will do. It captures every keystroke typed on a given keyboard. Now, if you were to examine the connection between your keyboard and the back of your computer, you would easily see an installed KeyKatch device. However, when was the last time that you actually examined the connections on your computer? Furthermore, KeyKatch looks like nothing more than a connector or plug and will usually be mistaken as being part of the computer / keyboard connection.

Someone with regular access to your computer (e.g., an office janitorial crew) with a couple of KeyKatch devices could grab 64,000 keystrokes of information per day from your computer. Simply install a KeyKatch device one day, switch it out the next day and download whatever information it contains, and repeat day after day.

Defeating these external keystroke-monitoring devices is simply a matter of preventing physical access to your computer and inspecting the connections between your keyboard and CPU to ensure that there are no extra devices installed. While you're thinking about it, take a minute to examine the connections on the back of your computer. Learn what is supposed to be there and then check regularly for any changes in this configuration.

CHAPTER 17

Password-Protect Your AOL Filing Cabinet

America Online (AOL) is one of the largest (if not the largest) Internet Service Providers in the world. The current version of AOL (Version 7.0) provides seven separate screen names (e-mail addresses), allowing each member of a family to have his or her own online address. The problem encountered by some families or other groups using AOL is that sent and received e-mail is stored in the AOL "filing cabinet," which is accessible offline by anyone who has access to the computer.

AOL provides a way to password-protect this filing cabinet so that that a password is required to access the stored e-mail even when you are offline. For some reason, many AOL users seem to have overlooked this additional security function.

If you want to add a password to your AOL filing cabinet, here's how to do it:

- Sign on to America Online with the screen name for which you want to create a filing cabinet password.

- On the AOL toolbar click on the Settings menu and then click Preferences.
- Under Account Controls in the Preferences window, click Passwords.
- Enter the password for your screen name in the Password box.
- Check the box for Filing Cabinet.

That's all there is to it. Now whenever you wish to access the filing cabinet under your AOL screen name (both online and offline), you will be prompted for your password.

Chapter 18

Add a JavaScript Password to Your Web Page

Many people establish personal Web pages, or even Web sites for a small business, on systems where they do not have control of the server that is hosting the site. If you have a page on America Online (AOL), or on one of the free sites such as Yahoo/GeoCities, you don't have control of the server, nor do you have access to CGI or the ability to set up security with such things as "htaccess." Still, you may want to add a "members only" section to your page or restrict access to certain individuals (e.g., family members).

One way of adding a password to a Web page where you don't control the server is by using JavaScript. Now I suspect that every computer programmer who reads this suggestion is choking on his coffee and screaming, "JavaScript isn't secure!" Fair enough. JavaScript doesn't provide a high level of security, and by all means, if you control the server where your Web page is hosted or have access to CGI or “htaccess,” use these functions instead. On the other hand, if, like many people establishing a Web page, you don’t have control of the server where it’s hosted, JavaScript offers at least some degree of security for your page.

You can think of JavaScript passwords much like the lock on the front door of the average home. It probably won’t require any great effort for a professional locksmith to bypass the lock, and professional burglars likely know a way to disable it, but it keeps most people out of your home. Likewise, it probably requires no great effort for a professional computer programmer to bypass a JavaScript password, and criminal computer hackers likely know a way to disable it, but it will keep most people out of the private areas of your Web page.

To set up a JavaScript password on your Web page, copy the following script into the html header of the page you want to protect. Edit the **BOLD, CAPITAL TEXT** as appropriate to reflect the password prompt, the password, and the messages you want to display when a correct or incorrect password is entered. The URL for the wrong password can send the user back to the log-in to try again or to any other location. A correct password, of course, grants access to the protected page.

```
<Script Language="JavaScript">
var passwd1 = prompt(' TYPE PASSWORD PROMPT TEXT HERE ',");
var passwd2 = " TYPE PASSWORD HERE ";
if (passwd1 == passwd2) {
alert(' TYPE CORRECT PASSWORD MESSAGE HERE '); }
else {
alert(' TYPE WRONG PASSWORD MESSAGE HERE ');
window.location=" HTTP://WRONG.PASSWORD.URL "; }
</Script>
```

The above JavaScript will keep the average computer user from accessing the protected area of your Web page. However, those with knowledge of how JavaScript works will realize that it is possible to bypass the password and access the page by turning off Java Scripting in their browser's security protocols. With Java Scripting turned off, when someone attempts to access your page, the password script does not run, but the remainder of the page is loaded and viewed.

To get around the problem of someone accessing your protected page by turning off Java Scripting, you can use JavaScript to redirect a user from a log-in page to the protected page. If Java Scripting is turned off when someone tries to go to the protected page, nothing happens because the protected page location is contained in the JavaScript itself. To set up a JavaScript redirect function, simply place the following JavaScript in the html header of a blank page and edit the URL so that it reflects the location of your protected page.

```
<Script Language="JavaScript">
<!–
window.location = "HTTP://PROTECTED-PAGE.URL";
// –>
</script>
```

By placing the above JavaScript on an intermediate "redirect" page between the public area of your Web page and the protected page on your site, you prevent someone from accessing your protected page by simply turning off Java Scripting. If someone clicks on the "members only" link from the public area of your Web page, the link sends them to your "redirect" page. If Java Scripting is working in his browser, he is automatically sent to your protected page and prompted for a password. If, however, he has Java Scripting turned off, the redirect script does not run, and he is stopped at the redirect page. You may choose to have some sort of message on the redirect page, such as an instruction that Java Scripting must be enabled to access the "members only" section.

With the redirect page in place and the JavaScript password on your protected page, you have stopped anyone from simply turning off Java Scripting in his browser in order to gain access to your protected page. However, it is still possible to bypass this setup.

To bypass the redirect page, one must go to the page with Java Scripting turned off. Of course, he will not be forwarded to the protected page. However, he can now use the View/Source function in his browser to look at the actual scripting of the page. This will reveal the URL of the protected page. It is now possible to go directly to the protected page, with Java Scripting turned off, and access the protected page without knowing the password.

You can defeat View/Source in a couple of ways. First it is possible to encrypt the redirect page so that anyone viewing source code on the page will not be able to recognize the URL it redirects to. There are several places on the Internet that allow you to download script encryption programs or to encrypt your script online. These programs are too complex to be of much value reproduced in a book (it would be a major headache trying to type in hundreds of lines of script from the text in a book). However you can easily find them on the Internet by searching "JavaScript and Encryption" on any major search engine.

The next method for defeating View/Source is to use a JavaScript where the URL of the protected page does not appear in the source code itself. In this case we use a simple script where the user is asked to log in. Once the log-in name is typed in, the JavaScript automatically appends the

".html" suffix to it and redirects to that page. For example, if the log in is "Skye," the JavaScript will redirect a legitimate visitor to http://www.domain.com/skye.html. But without knowledge of the log-in name (which is also the name of the protected page), a visitor can't access the page, and View/Source does not reveal the URL of the protected page because it is not contained in the source code itself. To use this type of log in/redirect, copy the following script into the header of your redirect page:

```
<Script Language="JavaScript">
<!–
var password = ''
password=prompt('Please enter your log in name:',");
if (password != null) {
location.href= password + ".html";
}
</Script>
```

You will note that the name of the protected page is not contained in this script. You just need to be sure that this redirect page and your protected page are contained in the same directory.

Using these simple JavaScripts will protect your Web page from many people browsing the Internet and from the merely curious. Of course, as you have seen, there are ways to bypass these simple JavaScript passwords, so you probably won't want to use them to safeguard your personal financial data or your plans to take over the world. However, if you want to post your family vacation photos and limit access to your family and friends (to whom you have given the password to your page), JavaScript may be the answer.

More complex and more secure JavaScript password protection scripts are available on the Internet, both as shareware and freeware. Once you are familiar with the basics of JavaScript password security, you may want to use more complex programs, or even write your own.

Chapter 19

Get Password Gates for Your Web Site

Restricting access to a Web site is fairly simple if you control the server on which the site is located and a bit of a challenge if you don't. When you don't control the server, one option is to use password gates.

The major Web support companies (such as Bravenet) provide password gates to enable you to establish password-controlled access to your Web site by directing authentication through their servers.

Unlike JavaScript password routines, a password gate can't be bypassed by simply turning off Java Scripting in the browser. However, once you have obtained the correct log-in and password once, you can simply bookmark the protected site and go directly to it thereafter. If you are using one of the free password gates, you will find that there is usually some kind of pop-up advertisement associated with the log-in procedure. This is usually not a major problem, and you are getting the password gate for free after all. Most of the password gates also allow you to get rid of the pop-up ads for a fee.

Some places to get a password gate for use on your Web site are listed below:

www.bravenet.com

www.4allfree.com

www.cgiforme.com

http://sethweb.frogspace.net/Simply_Secure/index.html

www.hits4me.com

www.sitegadgets.com

www.authpro.com

If you don't mind the pop-up ads (or are willing to pay the fee to get rid of them) and need a basic log-in/password for your Web site, password gates are definitely worth considering.

Part III

COUNTERING THREATS TO PRIVATE COMMUNICATIONS

CHAPTER 20

Encrypt Your E-Mail

For anyone who has a strong interest in or a definite need for online security, I recommend that you read my books *The Complete Guide to E-Security* and *Freeware Encryption and Security Programs*, both available from Paladin Press. These provide detailed discussions of encryption and online security. However, I believe using encryption to protect your e-mail is of such great importance that it should be mentioned briefly here also.

There are several good encryption programs (and some not so good) available online as freeware or through commercial sources. Of all the programs available, the one I recommend that everyone have is a free one called Pretty Good Privacy, or simply PGP.

PRETTY GOOD PRIVACY (PGP)

PGP is the unofficial Internet standard for e-mail encryption and online security. It is available as a free download from the Massachusetts Institute of Technology (MIT) distribution site at http://web.mit.edu/network/pgp.html

Once you have obtained a copy of PGP, you will need to install it on your computer (just like any other new program). During the installation and set-up procedure, you will make an encryption key pair. This consists of your "public key" and "secret key." Now you will provide a copy of your "public key," which allows encryption but not decryption, to others with PGP who may want to send you e-mail. You will obtain copies of the "public keys" of others so you can encrypt e-mail to them. Your "secret key," as the name implies, will always be kept secret, as it allows for decryption of messages encrypted with your "public key."

Here is an example of a PGP encrypted message:

——-BEGIN PGP MESSAGE——-
Version: PGP 6.0.2

qANQR1DDBFQDAAHJwKho/i2GM+ubMr6XmcvxyHKJTIoWJhdrfoAl+ecH8qtnI/8p
0bub7iq3Nbh4oCaaYnmZlVRtTn0v1cfVFpPdhvMX4bsrySThzGRcw60k3+vlCQ6i
/y74bh2/Fm6e5RZAk+LkmaMRknflMUhnQPywMm7hYdIZfHGme+xTsSaz3CMkLovd
UnLnbd1mAePwEfj5Nmp2h6vyhy0ielU2JfhGPaxZONpEVePng/gb9feefdHty7Gc
E53Mi4oB9vNKPaNrnpnusWtXxMpAIQS/4QIEZZJmQF+mvPqZWECzhjd8eUXqAdIf
gJhk3ey6tNjK080mpFDYg7ZUABS/xP+dXJFpqte54+083D+GDCWwDmvtwPpEuEiW
291LPDiHAl6NM2nDBtcfX98Tf8bv7YPwAeOPbkA9F1KqyvSyrr5j2BbYOrwAbXK2
H5DL8CBSoFsmRAE+CFU9lGeyFXvIAh9RisaHzS0/VdVtM3/EkfE=
=JQ2/
——-END PGP MESSAGE——-

As you can see, a message encrypted with PGP is totally unintelligible. Someone intercepting your e-mail will be unable to read it, and because PGP is a very strong encryption system it cannot be defeated by standard code-breaking methods.

If this all sounds too complicated, relax . . . it's not difficult at all. If you can install any new program on your computer, you can install PGP. The instructions included with PGP are very detailed. You will be able to send and receive secure e-mail within minutes after you have PGP installed. Furthermore, PGP contains several advanced security functions allowing you even greater security of your online communications and stored computer files.

If you do nothing else for your computer security, GET PGP!

ONE-WAY ENCRYPTION

The problem with using encryption programs is that they usually require a couple of extra keystrokes or an extra mouse click or two in order to implement their encryption / decryption functions. Unfortunately, the extra couple of seconds it takes to use encryption and secure your e-mail is more than some people are willing to spend. I have never really been able to understand this reluctance to use encryption when it is freely available and so easy to use. However, since this is too often the case, you can still secure your own e-mail by sending messages in self-decrypting archives, or as Web-based secure e-mail (such as www.ZipLip.com).

Using one-way encryption is not as secure as using a high-level encryption program such as PGP. However, it does offer more security than using nothing at all. To use one-way encryption, you will first create a message using some type of word processor or text editor. Then you will need to save this file as a password-secured file. This could be a password-protected Zip file, or if you're using a word-processor such as MS Word, you could use its built-in password function.

Attach this password-protected file to your e-mail and send it to your intended recipient. When he receives the message with the attached file and tries to open the file, he will be prompted to enter the password for this file. For this to be effective the person receiving the file must know what the password is in order to decrypt it. You can arrange this in advance or perhaps send some type of hint to the required password, but this weakens any security associated with using encryption.

If you are going to communicate regularly with someone via e-mail you should definitely have a strong encryption system established. For a one-time communication or an infrequent message via e-mail, one-way encryption is better than no encryption at all. However, if you are communicating with someone who refuses to use a secure means of communication you may want to reconsider whether you should be discussing anything private, personal, or of particular interest with this person. Even if he has no particular interest in security, he should respect your desire for privacy and personal security.

WHY BOTHER WITH ENCRYPTION?

When I suggest that people set up PGP or some other type of encryption to protect their e-mail, from time to time I get the response, "Why bother with encryption? I have nothing to hide." However, every one of these people with "nothing to hide" would almost certainly be upset to find the contents of their personal e-mail being posted to a public bulletin board or passed around the office. "I have nothing to hide" usually means "I don't believe anyone is snooping into my private e-mail, and I am too stupid and lazy to take reasonable precautions to protect myself and those with whom I communicate."

Even if you really do not care if all of your private e-mail is made public, are you sure that this holds true for everyone with whom you correspond? Even if you and all of your friends are glad to have your personal correspondence made public, there is still a very important reason to use encryption: it makes a strong statement in support of personal freedom and rightful liberty.

When you use encryption, you tell oppressive government agencies that they may not set up monitoring systems (Carnivore/DCS1000) on e-mail hubs to snoop into private communications. Encryption lets Big Brother know that you will not tolerate having the Constitution of the United States of America trampled underfoot in the name of expanding police powers.

I strongly believe that encrypted e-mail should be the standard, not the exception, in online communication. It is also important to note that once you set up an encryption system you should use it regularly. Even the most innocuous and mundane messages should be encrypted. If the only time you use encryption is when you have something of a confidential nature to discuss, the encryption itself raises a red flag. However, when all of your e-mail is encrypted, these messages and the fact that they are encrypted become innocuous.

Therefore, as a statement in support of our rightful liberty, Encrypt . . . encrypt . . . encrypt!

Chapter 21

Beware the Magic Lantern

After reading about keystroke monitoring (see Part II) and looking at the various keystroke-monitoring devices and programs, one might assume that these things are used by individuals trying to catch a cheating spouse, parents who are watching their children's activities online, and maybe even by some unscrupulous private investigators or overbearing employers. While this may all be true, perhaps the main purpose of keystroke monitoring is to defeat encryption programs.

If you use a strong encryption program and protect that program with a properly constructed password or pass-phrase, your private, encrypted information is very well protected from the various snoops, spies, and criminals who may try to access it. Unfortunately, although strong encryption algorithms can protect your private information, these encryption programs are generally accessed by using a password or pass-phrase. If someone discovers your password, he can decrypt your encrypted information, much like someone discovering the combination to your safe and being able to access its contents thereafter.

Notwithstanding former Secretary of State Henry Stimson's dictum that "gentlemen do not read each other's mail," our government has a very extensive program for snooping into our private communications. The FBI has its own keystroke-monitoring program called MAGIC LANTERN.

Now, MAGIC LANTERN is no real surprise to those of us who have an interest in personal privacy and believe strongly in the principles of the 4th Amendment. We saw the federal government attempt to destroy personal privacy with CLIPPER and CAPSTONE. Then we saw the deployment of CARNIVORE (later renamed DCS1000), the FBI's program for snooping into e-mail. As more and more people use encryption to protect the privacy of their e-mail, we now see MAGIC LANTERN being used by the federal government to invade that privacy.

On November 20, 2001, an MSNBC article by Bob Sullivan entitled "FBI Software Cracks Encryption Wall: 'Magic Lantern' part of new 'Enhanced Carnivore Project'" revealed the FBI's keystroke-monitoring scheme to the general public. Sullivan's article was quickly followed by similar Associated Press, *Boston Globe*, and *Washington Post* articles.

MAGIC LANTERN is simply a keystroke-monitoring program that can be installed on an individual's computer, thereafter transmitting every keystroke typed on said computer (including all passwords and access codes) to the feds!

MAGIC LANTERN is by definition a Trojan horse (as opposed to a computer virus) that is sent by the FBI to an individual (perhaps after co-opting the assistance of someone from whom that person regularly receives e-mail) with the idea that he will open the e-mail and run a "harmless" program, thereby installing MAGIC LANTERN on his computer.

You might assume that up-to-date antivirus software would detect a malicious program being surreptitiously installed on your computer. Apparently, however, the major antivirus companies are weakening their software to allow MAGIC LANTERN to slip by. According to a November 23, 2001, *Washington Post* article by Ted Bridis entitled "FBI Is Building a 'Magic Lantern': Software Would Allow Agency to Monitor Computer Use," "At least one company that makes antivirus software, McAfee.com Corp., contacted the FBI on Wednesday to ensure its software wouldn't inadvertently detect the bureau's snooping software and alert a criminal suspect."

So . . . if we must contend with the threat of keystroke monitoring from Big Brother and various other criminals, and the major antivirus software companies are weakening their programs so that all keystroke-monitoring programs to go undetected, just what do we do?

First, continue to use up-to-date antivirus software, but obtain it from companies that are not intentionally weakening their products. One company, "F-Secure" (www.europe.f-secure.com/index.shtml) in Finland, offers excellent products and has no particular reason to make them less effective to support an FBI eavesdropping scheme. It should be noted that F-Secure is an international company with offices in the United States, so there is some potential for Big Brother to influence it, but as of this writing I am not aware of F-Secure's adding specific weaknesses and vulnerabilities to its software.

Most effective in defeating keystroke monitoring, however, is using strong encryption (e.g., PGP, TWOFISH, etc.) to send and receive all e-mail, but doing all encrypting and decrypting on a separate, secure computer. This is a standard procedure within agencies that deal with "classified" information. All processing of classified or proprietary information is conducted on a separate, secure computer.

You can establish the same type of security by using a separate stand-alone computer to work on any sensitive documents and to write all private e-mail. Using PGP (or some other strong encryption program), you then encrypt any documents that need to be transmitted and save these documents to a floppy disk (or other removable media). These encrypted documents are then transferred from the floppy disk to your computer connected to the Internet. Encrypted e-mail received on your Internet computer is saved to disk and transferred to your secure computer.

It is important to be certain that you only transfer text files to your secure computer from your Internet computer. NEVER TRANSFER A PROGRAM! Remember MAGIC LANTERN and other harmful Trojan horses and viruses can be contained in any type of an executable file (program), but not in a text file. It is also essential that you take great care to protect your secure computer from physical access. Keep it with you, or keep it locked in a safe, but protect it!

Because all encryption and decryption, as well as all sensitive work, is performed on your secure computer, there is no way for a keystroke capture program to transmit your passwords to some snoop on the Internet. You never type any passwords or work with any plain-text sensitive information on your Internet computer.

This may seem like a lot of extra effort (and it is) to protect the security of your sensitive documents and communications. However, these types of procedures are standard among those individuals and agencies that deal with classified and proprietary information. If you have information of such significant interest to others that they may employ keystroke monitoring to get it, you will need to employ these countermeasures to ensure that their attacks fail.

CHAPTER 22

Prevent Telephone Monitoring with Digital Spread Spectrum

If you are using an analog cordless or cellular telephone, someone is listening to your telephone conversations! You'll notice I did not say someone *might* be listening to your telephone conversations, or there is a *possibility* that your telephone conversations can be overheard. Simply put, your telephone conversations are being monitored! Radio hobbyists with their scanners have the capability to listen to telephone conversations, and we must assume that a small percentage do from time to time. Beyond these hobbyists, however, is an underground culture of scanner users who make specific efforts to monitor telephone conversations. This underground culture ranges from individuals wanting nothing more than to satisfy their personal curiosity, to news reporters looking for leads, to private eyes gathering information for a case, to criminals listening for credit card numbers, SSNs, or other information to be used in the furtherance of a crime. Beyond this, various law enforcement and security agencies may monitor telephones for their own purposes.

But wait, you say—it's illegal to monitor telephone conversations. It's even illegal for the police to do so without a warrant. True, it's illegal to monitor telephone conversations, but do you really think that no one's listening? A law is nothing more than words and, in and of itself, does nothing to prevent that which it proscribes. The chances of getting caught monitoring telephone conversations are almost nil, and when have you ever heard of anyone being prosecuted for monitoring a cordless telephone?

One way to prevent monitoring of your telephone conversations is through the use of digital spread spectrum technology. To understand this, we first need to be aware that telephones are either analog or digital. Analog telephones are nothing more than radio transmitters sending signals between the telephone and the cell site in the case of cellular telephones and between the handset and the base in the case of cordless telephones. Cellular telephones operate on 832 frequency pairs with 30 KHz spacing in the 824.04 MHz–893.97 MHz range, and cordless telephones operate in the 43.720 MHz–49.990 MHz range, the 902.00 MHz–927.900 MHz range, and the 2.4 GHz range. Any radio scanner can be programmed to receive the cordless telephone frequencies. Newer scanners have the cellular telephone frequencies block, but these frequencies can be unblocked by anyone with a basic knowledge of radio electronics. Digital telephones are also radio transmitters, but a digital signal is unintelligible when heard on an analog receiver. Of course, a digital receiver would receive a digital telephone signal were it programmed to the appropriate frequency. However, here is where spread spectrum technology comes in.

Spread spectrum technology is not a new concept. In fact, the basic concept was patented by actress Hedy Lamarr and used during World War II as a method to prevent torpedoes from being jammed en route to their target. The concept stayed within the military realm until 1983 when the Federal Communications Commission (FCC) authorized its commercial use.

Digital spread spectrum uses a broadband signal spread over a number of frequencies. These signals are difficult to intercept and demodulate and are resistant to jamming or interference. This provides for a clearer and cleaner telephone signal, as well as preventing monitoring of the signal itself. It is also worth noting that cordless telephones are now available with an operating frequency of 2.4 GHz. Since most scanners do not receive into the gigahertz range, this gives additional protection against interception of your telephone signal as it is transmitted between the handset and the base.

Chapter 23

Install a Scrambler on Your Telephone Line

If someone is actively targeting you, attempting to gather information for whatever purpose, it is almost guaranteed that your cordless and cellular telephone conversations are being listened to (and it is quite likely that there will be an effort to tap your hard-wired telephone as well—more on that in a bit).

If you are using a digital cordless telephone with spread spectrum technology, you can be fairly confident that the signal between the handset and the base isn't being monitored. If you are using the newer digital cellular service, you can likewise have confidence that your conversation is not being monitored between your telephone and the cell site. However, once your cordless telephone sends a signal from the base down the telephone line, you no longer have a digital spread spectrum signal, and your digital cellular telephone will switch to an analog signal as soon as you enter a roaming area outside of the digital service area.

With this in mind, you may wish to install a telephone (voice) scrambler on your line to secure your sensitive conversations. Doing so will prevent any casual listener from monitoring your conversations, and, depending on what type of scrambler you use, it may prevent even Big Brother from making sense of your telephone calls.

Secure telephones were once the domain of the military, government agencies, and major corporations. However, today the very best telephone voice scrambler units (such as the STU-III), costing just a few thousand dollars each, are available to the commercial market. Voice scramblers may be divided into the following broad categories:

Frequency Inversion—Frequency inversion is the simplest form of voice scrambling and just inverts the high and low points in the signal. Using a pivot point of around 3,300 hertz, frequency inversion reverses the high and low frequencies around this point. This gives a Donald Duck-like sound to the scrambled signal. Some writers have stated that a "trained ear" could determine what was being said in a frequency inversion scrambled signal, but this seems unlikely. I have listened to this type of scrambled signal and find it unintelligible, and I have never spoken to anyone who could actually determine what was being said in the scrambled signal. Still, I suppose there may be someone somewhere who can understand frequency-inverted speech.

You can purchase a frequency inversion scrambler for around $100 or, if you have basic electronics skills, build one for about $30. Along the same lines, you can build the decoder, which will quickly defeat a simple frequency inversion voice scrambler. If you are simply trying to keep someone from listening in on your conversation on an extension, this type of voice scrambler will work, but anyone who puts any effort into defeating the frequency inversion will have little trouble doing so.

Rolling Code—Rolling-code voice scramblers also use frequency inversion but add an additional function so that the pivot point around which the frequency is scrambled is continuously changing. This makes decoding of the signal much more difficult. If you listen to a signal scrambled with rolling code, you will hear a data burst at the beginning of the connection as the scramblers synchronize their code with a session key and operator preset key. Because someone trying to eavesdrop on this conversation will not be able to match the rolling code, he will not be able to decode it in the same way as can be done with simple frequency inversion. Some manufacturers of rolling-code scramblers have switched to a frequency-hopping as opposed to rolling code, offering an even greater degree of security against unauthorized decoding of the signal.

By using a rolling-code scrambler you will secure your conversations against any casual listeners, criminal eavesdroppers, and local investigators and law enforcement agencies. The rolling-code scramblers are in about the same price range as the basic frequency-inversion scramblers. This gives reasonable security at affordable prices.

One company offering a wide range of scramblers, from the simplest frequency-inversion type to high-security digital encryption models, is Transcrypt Secure Technologies (www.transcrypt-secure.com).

Digital Encryption—Digital-encryption scramblers are the most secure and the most expensive. These scramblers are made by such major corporations as AT&T and Motorola and are used by the military, government agencies, and major corporations to secure their communications. This type of scrambler starts around $1,500 and goes up in price from there. If you are concerned about having your telephone calls intercepted by government agencies or are afraid of industrial espionage, digital encryption is the only answer, but for most of us the sensitivity of our conversations does not require this level of security and the associated expense.

An exception to the high-cost digital encryption scramblers is the Privatel voice scrambler, with a price tag of $595 at the time of this writing. Privatel is made by Communications Systems-East (www.L-3com.com/privatel) and uses the 3-DES algorithm and a session key exchange for very effective high-level security.

It is important to remember that you must have a voice scrambler on each end of the conversation and that scrambling your voice on the telephone line does not defeat an electronic listening device that is placed to intercept room audio.

Now, while I have said that a scrambler must be on each end of the conversation, there is a bit of an exception to this. There is a technique called "vulnerable-path encryption" that encrypts half of the communications path, or what is considered the vulnerable path. Let's say that you will be traveling and plan to receive calls on your cellular telephone. We have already seen that cellular and cordless telephones are monitored in their analog mode. To defeat this monitoring, you receive your calls through your home telephone (or other hard-wired telephone) and use call forwarding to connect to your cellular telephone. Place a voice scrambler on your cellular telephone and on your home telephone, thereby scrambling the portion of the call that is transmitted on the monitored cellular frequencies (the vulnerable path). It is important to set this system up so that calls to your landline telephone are actually redialed and call your cellular telephone. Call forwarding, which simply redirects from the landline-dialed telephone number to your cellular telephone number, will not allow the encryption path to work. Of course, the portion of the telephone call going from your home telephone over the telephone lines is not encrypted, but it is also not being broadcast on the monitored cellular frequencies. To employ this technique you must use scramblers that perform automatic synchronization, but then all but the cheapest scramblers do this, so vulnerable-path encryption is a technique that works fairly well.

Chapter 24

Be Selective in Purchasing Telephone Voice-Changers

Telephone voice-changers are devices that connect in line with your telephone (or complete telephones with voice-changing circuits built in) that allow you to change the sound of your voice as it's sent over the telephone line, thus making your voice unrecognizable to the person on the other end of the line. The companies marketing these voice-changers say that you can use them to give the impression that more than one person is home when you are home alone. You can also change your voice to make inquiries or comments where you might be known or later recognized by the sound of your voice.

Unfortunately, most of the voice-changing telephone devices simply use a sliding scale to allow you to alter the pitch of your voice, giving you the option of sounding like Daffy Duck or the Dark Overlord of the Universe. Your voice will be unrecognizable, but it will also be obvious that you are doing something to alter it. Only the most gullible will believe that this altered voice is the normal voice of another person.

Quite simply, when it comes to telephone voice-changers, "you get what you pay for." It is certainly possible to electronically modify your voice to have the sound quality of another normal human voice, but it just doesn't happen for $19.95. If you have a serious need to electronically alter your voice on the telephone, you can purchase a voice-changer from Shomer-Tec, Inc. (www.shomer-tec.com) called the Telephone Voice Transformer for about $500. This device will let you electronically modify the sound of your voice to take on the sound of another normal human voice, but it will cost you 10 times more than the voice-changers seen elsewhere that let you do a great impression of Daffy Duck.

I believe that the voice-changing telephone is of limited value as a security device. My reasoning for this is a matter of cost versus benefit. For a voice-changing telephone to be effective, you will have to spend a few hundred dollars. The number of times you would telephone someone who could recognize your voice when you do not want to be identified should be almost nil.

The one exception I make to using a voice-changing telephone is if you have a concern about voice print technology. During the past few years there have been significant advances in the voice recognition capabilities of computer systems. There are currently security systems on the market that utilize voiceprints to authenticate selected individuals. This same technology can be used to scan large groups of intercepted telephone calls in order to locate the one made by a selected individual. Voice-changing telephones will offer some degree of countermeasure against voiceprint tracking.

Chapter 25

Research Bug Detectors Carefully

There are various spy shops and some security companies that sell devices intended to let the user detect electronic surveillance devices (bugs) on their telephone line or in a room. The cost of these "bug detectors" ranges from a couple hundred dollars up to several thousand dollars. But the question that must be asked is, *do they work*? The answer is a qualified, yes . . . no . . . and maybe.

If you are hoping to use these bug detectors to detect FBI telephone intercept installed at the local telephone company central switching office, you are simply out of luck. They do *not* work. If your telephone line is tapped by some agency with access to the telephone company central switch, you will not be able to detect it. There will be no clicks or funny humming noise on your line, no mysterious rings, and no background voices. That only happens in the movies and spy novels. Central switch monitoring can be defeated through encryption, but there is no sure way to detect these taps.

On the other hand, if you are hoping to detect someone listening in on an extension line, or some James Bond wannabe who has clipped a tape recorder somewhere on your local line, these detectors work fairly well.

In addition to those that detect telephone-monitoring devices, there are devices available that will detect room bugs that have been placed to record room audio. Here again, if you are trying to detect professionally placed devices with a few hundred dollars worth of equipment, good luck; I wouldn't hold out much hope for success here. On the other hand, if you are in search of a Radio Shack special put together by a jealous spouse or some amateur detective, you may have some success.

The first line of defense against room bugs is physical security. Simply don't allow anyone the access needed to plant the bug in the first place. A detailed physical search will often detect room bugs (but not always). Room audio (i.e., playing a radio or other noise) can also help defeat them. Many agencies concerned about the possibility of electronic listening devices play "cover music" in their offices. This isn't for the entertainment of their employees but to help mask conversation and to keep any listening device in an "always-on" position, thereby draining batteries and making electronic detection of the device easier.

The short answer on "bug detectors" is that they will offer a defense against the amateur eavesdropper but are almost useless against professional investigators and Big Brother. If you are a businessman concerned about competitive intelligence (industrial espionage), I strongly recommend that you hire a professional countermeasures company to evaluate the threat to your company and assist you in developing a protective posture.

One of the best countermeasures companies in the business is Murray Associates.

Even if you are only concerned about amateur snoops, I recommend that you take a look at the Murray Associates Web site (www.spybusters.com). The page contains a lot of very useful information about electronic monitoring and countermeasures thereto. Just developing knowledge of countermeasures technology will help you evaluate the threat and aid you in planning your own countermeasures.

Chapter 26

Use Prepaid Telephone Calling Cards

Use of a prepaid calling card is another way of obtaining some degree of privacy in your telephone communications. These calling cards, which are available most everywhere, give you a certain number of calling minutes based on the cost of the card.

When you use a prepaid calling card, you are provided with a toll-free access number and a calling card number. Dial the access number, enter your calling card number and the number you want to be connected to, and your call goes through. The length of your call is deducted from the number of minutes available on the calling card. This is all done within the computer system of the calling card company, so you don't actually need physical possession of the prepaid calling card. All you need is knowledge of the access number for the calling card and the card number itself.

It is also interesting to note that in some cases use of a calling card will mask your number to Caller ID. This is not always the case, but as with calls through a PBX

(Private Branch Exchange, or private telephone network), Caller ID may see only the calling card computer system and not your originating number.

It is important to remember that the number from which you access the prepaid calling card service will become part of the company's records, as will the number you call. Be aware that these records may be able to show a link between you and the person you called if you do something foolish, such as accessing the calling card from your home telephone.

Chapter 27

Use Prepaid Cellular Telephone Service

A good option to obtain a degree of telephone privacy is to use prepaid cellular service. This is not particularly new; it has been available at airports for years, enabling customers to swipe a credit card at a vending machine and receive a cellular telephone with a given number of prepaid minutes available for use.

Prepaid cellular service is also available from major office supply stores and many electronics stores. Whereas a prepaid cellular telephone purchased from an airport vending machine links the customer to the telephone through the credit card transaction, prepaid cellular service can be purchased with cash in an office supply store.

When purchasing a prepaid cellular service, you will receive a basic cellular telephone and choose a number of minutes with which to begin your service (usually you are given the choice of 100 minutes, 300 minutes, 800 minutes, 1,500 minutes, or similar blocks of minutes). Pay for the package you want and you are given an activation number to set up your service. Call the number. Respond to the various prompts to activate your phone, and you have cellular service. The security/privacy advantage you have is that this telephone is not linked to you by name, address, credit card number, etc.

Your prepaid cellular telephone will work like any other cellular service. You have a telephone number and can make and receive calls. It is important to remember that once you use the telephone, calls made from it can be linked to that specific telephone, though there is no record of who actually has the telephone itself.

In setting up the prepaid cellular service you are assigned a telephone number from a bank of numbers used by the service provider. As long as you continue to use the service, you keep the same telephone number. You can add additional minutes of service to your prepaid cellular service by purchasing them with a credit card (which totally defeats any anonymity you had) or with cash at an office supply store or wherever you obtained the service to begin with. However, if you do not use your cellular service for a few weeks (usually 30 to 90 days), you lose your assigned number and must reactivate your telephone before you can use it again. You will still have the remaining unused minutes of your prepaid cellular service, but your assigned telephone number will likely change.

The fact that your cellular telephone number changes after a given period of nonuse of the service may actually be an advantage in some circumstances. It is important to remember, however, that the electronic serial number (ESN) that is transmitted as part of every cellular telephone call does not change. So calls can still be linked to your specific telephone—and to you if you are in possession of the telephone.

Prepaid cellular is an excellent service. When purchased with cash, it gives you all the advantages of cellular service without the intrusiveness of the service contracts associated with standard cellular service.

CHAPTER 28

Purchase Caller ID, Line Blocking, and Other Telephone Services

Most telephone companies offer various options you can include with your basic service. Many of these services are useful from a privacy/countermeasures standpoint. Let's take a look at a few of them.

UNLISTED/UNPUBLISHED NUMBER

Having an unlisted/unpublished telephone number has significant privacy advantages. The most obvious of these is that you don't appear in the local telephone directory and directory assistance (information) will not disclose your telephone number. There is no sense letting just anyone locate you by simply looking in the telephone directory.

Having an unlisted telephone number will also significantly reduce the number of calls you get from telemarketers. Unfortunately, it will not totally eliminate this invasion of your home's privacy, since many telemarketers will simply dial every possible number in a given exchange, but it will reduce the calls considerably.

It will probably cost you no more than a dollar per month to have an unlisted telephone number, a dollar I believe to be well spent for the privacy advantages of not being listed in the telephone directory.

You should be aware, however, that even though your telephone number does not appear in the telephone directory, it may in time end up on other telephone lists and databases. Your telephone number can be obtained from various records into which you may enter it. So be aware of where you disclose your unlisted telephone number.

CALLER ID

Of all the services offered by the telephone company, I tend to like Caller ID the most. It is nice to know who's calling before picking up the telephone. The most basic form of Caller ID will just display the number from which the incoming call originated. More advanced Caller ID also displays the name associated with the originating number and perhaps stores this information, along with the date and time of the call, in a "call list." Unfortunately, not all numbers will be displayed accurately on Caller ID. Calls made through a PBX often don't display accurately, and calls from out of your calling area may not display the number, but overall, Caller ID is a good service to have.

CALL BLOCKING (#67)

With Caller ID comes the fact that many people do not want to have their telephone number (and perhaps name) revealed when they make a call to someone using Caller ID. To prevent this information from being displayed on Caller ID systems, the telephone company offers Call

Blocking. You can activate this feature, on a per-call basis, by dialing a given code (usually *67) before making a call. This prevents Caller ID information from being transmitted with your phone call. A Caller ID box will display "private," "anonymous," "unavailable," or a similar message. Usually you can also have this Call Blocking feature added to your line (per-line blocking) so that all your calls have Call Blocking added without the need to dial *67. The per-line blocking feature may, however, cost you an extra dollar per month with the phone company.

It is important to remember that Call Blocking does *not* block caller information from being sent to calls made to 911, toll-free numbers (1-800, 877, etc.), and pay-per-call (900 series) numbers.

ANONYMOUS CALL REJECTION (*77)

As the battle between Caller ID and Call Blocking continues, an option called Anonymous Call Rejection has been added to the mix. In this case, if someone calls you using Call Blocking he receives a message stating that you do not accept blocked calls and that he will have to unblock his number in order for the call to go through. While this feature will ensure that Caller ID information is provided with any call to your home, it does disclose the fact that you have Caller ID in place. The fact that I use Caller ID is no secret, so I have anonymous call rejection active on my phone line. This gives me a record of any calls made to my home. I generally prefer the advantage of knowing who has called over keeping that fact that I have Caller ID a secret.

CHAPTER 29

Use a "Call Filter"

Do you get an annoying number of telemarketing calls? Is someone harassing you over the telephone? These types of calls can be maddening, but what can you do about it? Yes, you can get a new telephone number and have it unpublished, but if someone got your current number he may be able to get your new number, and unpublished numbers do nothing to stop telemarketers who simply call every possible number in a given telephone exchange. Of course, you can just disconnect your telephone, but then you receive no calls whatsoever. You probably still want to receive calls from friends and family but also want to enjoy the privacy of your home without unwelcome interruptions. Some telephone companies offer privacy services that help protect you against telemarketers and other unwelcome calls, but this option adds an additional monthly fee to your phone bill and is not all that effective against a determined caller.

There is a device that allows you to take control of your telephone privacy by adding an access code to your telephone number before it will ring. This device is marketed as a "call filter" or "telephone privacy filter" and is a small box that connects to your telephone line between the wall and the telephone itself (much like an answering machine). You choose a 4-digit access code, setting it on the call filter. Turn the call filter on, and when someone dials your number he will hear an automated voice saying, "Thank you for calling. Please enter your access code to complete this call." If the person then enters the 4-digit code you have set, your telephone will ring. If he doesn't enter the correct access code, he is disconnected. The call filter also has an on/off switch, letting you turn the device off and thereby allow your telephone to function normally. Want a little privacy? Turn the call filter on, and only those close friends to whom you have provided your access code can call you. Because you can set your own access code, should your code ever be obtained by someone from whom you don't want to receive calls, just set a new code. Call filters are sold by various electronics stores and spy shops; just search online for "telephone call filter." Prices vary quite a bit, but the best deal I have found is from Bellingham, Washington-based Shomer-Tec, which listed the Telephone Privacy Filter for $49 in its 2002 catalog.

CHAPTER 30

Fight Postal Service Abuses

The U.S. Postal Service (USPS) generally does a fairly good job of delivering the mail in a timely manner. Although our postal rates tend to go up by a cent or two every couple of years, the cost of postage in the United States is still much lower than in many other countries.

Unfortunately, however, there is no real privacy associated with our addresses or our mail. When you rent a box at your local post office, you will be required to fill out a form providing your name and street address. You will then be required to present two pieces of identification, one of which must be photo ID. The postal clerk renting the box to you will confirm that the information on the post office box rental application matches that on the identification presented and will record the type of ID presented on the application itself.

This intrusive demand for photo ID has become commonplace among government and quasi-government agencies. Demanding photo ID from someone who wants a private mailbox (as opposed to a mailbox for conducting business with the public) seems somewhat unnecessary to me. However, the real problem comes about when the USPS does little to safeguard the information it has gathered from its customers.

The job of the postal service is to deliver the mail, and to be fair it does a fairly good job of this. However, the postal service is also in the business of spying on us. When you provide information to the postal service to rent a post office box or have mail delivered to your home, you probably intend for that information to be used solely to deliver your mail. Yet, if you fill out a change of address card to have your mail forwarded to a new address, you will soon find that you are being swamped with junk mail from a number of direct marketers. Why? Because the postal service provides data in its National Change of Address (NCOA) database to direct marketers.

Even if you aren't planning a move in the near future with the associated change of address, the information you provided the postal service to have your mail delivered to your current address is not protected from disclosure. It's available to government agencies and many semiofficial private agencies with little effort. According to Deputy Director J. Bradley Jansen of the Center for Technology Policy at the Free Congress Foundation, "The United States Postal Service has an abysmal privacy record, and the American people deserve far better privacy protection than they receive."

OK, so the postal service may not be the National Security Agency when it comes to secrecy, but if all it's doing is distributing your address information, is this really such a problem? Well, yes it is. The postal service should not be using your private information for the commercial benefit of direct marketers, but this is just the tip of its privacy-crushing iceberg.

Since 1997, the postal service has been conducting a program specifically designed to report on the activities of postal customers. This program is called "Under the Eagle Eye." Under this program, postal clerks are required to report "suspicious activity" of customers to law enforcement. The postal service is very closemouthed about just what it considers "suspicious activity" but admits that this suspicious activity may include such things as purchasing a large money order or buying several smaller-denomination money orders or counting cash while waiting in line at the post office.

According to Congressman Ron Paul (R-Texas), the training manual for the Under the Eagle Eye program explicitly states that "it is better to report many legitimate transactions that seem suspicious than to let one illegal one slip through." Commenting on the postal service's policy, Congressman Paul says, "This policy turns the presumption of innocence, which has been recognized as one of the bulwarks of liberty since medieval times on its head. Allowing any federal employee to assume the possibility of a crime based on nothing more than a subjective judgment of 'suspicious behavior' represents a serious erosion of our constitutional rights to liberty, privacy, and due process."

Because of the lack of privacy within the USPS, many people opt to use commercial mail-receiving agencies such as Mail Boxes Etc. These companies act like private post offices, providing not only mailboxes but also expanded services not available at U.S. post offices (e.g., the ability to receive packages from private couriers such as UPS and Federal Express).

Initially, commercial mail-receiving agencies allowed customers to structure their addresses to give the appearance of a residence or office by listing their box number as Apt. # or Suite #. Furthermore, ID requirements were minimal as long as customers paid their box fees. However, in 1999 the USPS changed the rules, requiring all commercial mail-receiving agencies to gather privacy-invading information from their customers. Anyone who wishes to rent a private mailbox must now show two forms of identification to verify a permanent address, a telephone number, and a "serial number" traceable to the renter. (This serial number is often a driver's license number, but too often it ends up being one's SSN!) How can the postal service do this, asked the CMRAs (and their customers) when they found that Big Brother was disrupting their business and infringing on privacy rights. Simply put, the postal service has certain regulatory powers. Thus, disregarding all public comment protesting its actions, it simply established regulations that make it illegal for a CMRA to receive mail for an individual if said individual has not filled out the forms, presented the ID, and complied with the postal service's intrusive requirements. The postal service refused to deliver mail to the CMRAs unless they complied with these regulations. If a CMRA sought to protect the privacy of its customers and declined to require that they provide the information demanded by the postal service, the CMRA was simply put out of business. After all, you can't be a commercial mail-receiving agency if you can't receive mail for your customers!

The USPS also mandated a change in the address format used by commercial mail-receiving agencies. Under the new rules, "Box #," "Apt. #," and "Suite #" had to be replaced with the designation "PMB #," for Private Mail Box number. Again, the USPS went so far as to refuse to deliver mail that did not contain the PMB designation, even though it may have been delivering to that same address for years.

According the USPS, these intrusive ID requirements were implemented for the purpose of fighting mail fraud—

the idea being that credit card companies, loan companies, and the like would know that they were sending mail to a private mailbox and not a residential or business physical address. But this reasoning simply doesn't make much sense. Since 1994 the USPS has included a "check digit" in the bar code of private mailbox addresses. Simply put, major institutional mailers had, for five years prior to the new USPS regulation, had the ability to differentiate between addresses that were associated with a commercial mail-receiving agency and those that were not. Furthermore, there was no real evidence that commercial mail-receiving agencies were used for mail fraud purposes to any greater degree than P.O. boxes or other types of addresses.

As is the case with most government regulations, there was a period of time set aside for public comment on this new USPS scheme before it became "law." The postal service received 10 (yes, 10!) comments in favor of the new regulations affecting commercial mail-receiving agencies. On the other hand, it received 8,107 comments opposing the new regulations. That's 800 to 1 against the new regulations, but did USPS listen? Of course not, the regulations were implemented at an estimated cost of $900 million to the CMRAs. Not only did the new law cause commercial mail-receiving agencies to lose business, but it put at risk the privacy of those using private mailboxes for personal safety reasons (such as victims of domestic violence seeking to shield their location for from abusive partners and stalkers).

It is common knowledge that if you file a permanent change-of-address card with the USPS it will provide your new address to mailers and to major companies receiving the National Change of Address (NCOA) list. (However, you are not added to the NCOA list if you file a temporary change of address.) But if you receive your mail through a commercial mail-receiving agency, just what information will the USPS release, and to whom? Well, if you file a change-of-address card, it works pretty much the same way no matter where you receive your mail. To find out exactly what information the USPS will release if you are using the services of a commercial mail-receiving agency, you need only read the Privacy Act information contained on the back of PS Form 1582, which the USPS requires you to fill out before it will deliver your mail to such an agency:

> *The Postal Service may disclose this information to an appropriate government agency, domestic or foreign, for law enforcement purposes; where pertinent, in a legal proceeding to which the Postal Service is a party or has an interest; to a government agency in order to obtain information relevant to a USPS decision concerning employment, security clearances, contracts, licenses, grants, or other benefits; to a congressional office at your request; to an expert, consultant, or other person under contract to the USPS to fulfill an agency function; to the Federal Records Center for storage; to the Office of Management and Budget for review of private relief legislation; to an independent certified public accountant during an official audit of USPS finances; to a labor organization as required by the National Labor Relations Act; for the purpose of identifying an address as an address of an agent to whom mail is delivered on the behalf of other persons; and to anyone when the delivery address is being used for the purpose of doing or soliciting business with the public.*

In other words, the USPS will disclose your private information to pretty much everyone! Also, you should be aware that most federal agencies can access the information stored in the Federal Records Centers without a warrant or even any particularly good reason. The Federal Records Center is maintained by the National Archives and Records Administration. It maintains a vast number of records on file for the purpose of public disclosure, as well as records that are not intended for public disclosure but are available to government agencies and agents. In my 20+ years of government service (most of it in counterintelligence), I often made requests to other agencies for information needed for whatever project I was working on at the time. In all that time, I never had an agency tell me that I couldn't have access to a record because the record contained private information about an individual. No agency ever told me to get a warrant to access records or asked for much more than a memorandum from my office requesting a particular record or access to a specific database.

So while commercial mail-receiving agencies were once quite useful for privacy, the current USPS regulations make them much less so. But there are ways to fight this government invasion of privacy. Because the USPS will not deliver mail addressed to someone at a commercial mail-receiving agency unless that person fills out a PS Form 1582 and structures his address to contain the PMB designation, you can cause a little misdirection and confusion for anyone trying to track you down. When you change mailing addresses (notice I did not necessarily say that you have actually moved), you should never fill out a permanent postal change-of-address card with your new address. Doing so simply gets you entered into the NCOA database. Instead, simply contact whomever you want to have your new mailing address directly!

Now, if you just close out your P.O. box or private mailbox and leave no forwarding address, mail sent to your old address will be returned to sender indicating that the mail is undeliverable and you left NO FORWARDING ADDRESS. However, you can give the impression that you have moved to sunny southern California by filling out a permanent change-of-address card with the address of a commercial mail-receiving agency in . . . let's say, Hollywood. Simply look up the address of a commercial mail-receiving agency in Hollywood and list its street address as your new address on the USPS change-of-address card. If you need help finding the addresses of commercial mail-receiving agencies, Mail Boxes Etc. has a Web site (www.mbe.com) that lists all of its store locations. So your new address looks something like this:

John Q. Public
000 Hollywood Blvd. Apt. 123
Hollywood, CA 90028

Because this address does not contain the PMB designation, mail sent there will be returned to the sender marked "UNDELIVERABLE—Commercial Mail Receiving Agency—No Authorization to Receive Mail for This Addressee." Instead of "Addressee Unknown" or "No Forwarding Address," this says that the CMRA is not authorized to receive mail for you. Any inquiries about the returned mail at the sender's local post office will likely be answered with an explanation about the required PMB designation in the address. It's now up to the sender to figure out whether the address is bogus or whether USPS regulations and bureaucracy are simply preventing you from getting your mail.

But is there any way to ensure some degree of privacy in receiving mail? Well, although it is illegal to provide false information on federal forms, it would certainly be *possible* to obtain a post office box or private mailbox using alternate ID. Someone presenting a fake out-of-state driver's license and some in-state secondary ID at the post office when renting a P.O. box as a new resident in the state would have little difficulty obtaining that box. After all, the postal clerk is probably no more aware of what driver's licenses from other states look like than anyone else. Once the box is obtained it could be maintained for years without any question as long as the rental fees were paid on time. But again, it's illegal to lie to Big Brother, so I can't advise you to take this route.

You can, of course, rent a P.O. box (or a private mailbox) under your own name, using valid government-issued photo ID, jumping through all the bureaucratic hoops, and filling out all the information demanded on the forms. But it's conceivable that at some future point you might move to a nearby town. As things change over the months and years, many people "forget" to update various bureaucratic forms filled out months or years before. In the event that this happened in your case, your P.O. box would no longer be associated with your new street address. The two pieces of ID that you originally recorded in block 9 of PS Form 1093 (Application for Post Office Box or Caller Service) could still be used to track you down, of course. But by not having your current street address associated with your P.O. box, you add one more layer of the "onionskin" to your personal privacy measures.

By declaring war against the commercial mail-receiving agencies, the USPS invaded our privacy at a cost of millions of dollars. There was no legitimate reason for this, and it certainly harmed people who needed these private and specialized mail services.

There are several groups of people who need such specialized mail services, including business travelers, RVers, merchant marines and other commercial sailors, long-haul truckers, and other perpetual travelers. Some of these groups have organizations set up to support their lifestyles. They provide mail receiving and forwarding services, messaging services, and many other services for their members and clients. A couple of examples of these organizations are:

Escapees RV Club (www.escapees.com)
Voyager's Mail Forwarding Service (http://vmfs.com)

Because these groups are commercial ventures, they tend to get caught up in the bureaucracy, red tape, and regulations of the USPS. However, a small mutual support group of individuals interested in maintaining their individual sovereignty and personal privacy could do much the same thing without the problems faced by a commercial agency!

Interestingly enough, I served as the secretary of a private club for a couple of years. The club received mail at a P.O. box. On the PS Form 1093 (Application for Post Office Box or Caller Service), we answered "Yes" to the question, "Will this box be used for soliciting or doing business with the public?" Thus, the post office would disclose the "street address" of the club to anyone who asked. However, this really wasn't much of a secret. I found that because this was a "business box," the post office would deliver mail to the box regardless of the personal name on the mail, as long as the box number was correct. I checked with the postmaster, and he had no objection whatsoever to this. Thus, any club member could receive mail at the club address and have the mail held for him at the club. There was no requirement for any list of names authorized to receive mail at the club's P.O. box. In the space for recording the names of those authorized to receive mail at the P.O. box, the postmaster simply put "ALL / ANY NAMES."

We even set up a procedure whereby the club would forward mail to its members when they were away. Any club member who wished to receive mail at the club and have it forwarded to another address would place on file with the club secretary a number of prestamped USPS Priority Mail Flat Rate Envelopes. (At the time of this writing, the Flat Rate Envelope allows one to send as much mail as one can stuff into the envelope for a flat rate of $3.95.) Mail received at the club for a given member would be placed in the envelope and mailed wherever the member directed on a weekly, biweekly, or monthly basis.

Someone attempting to locate an individual receiving mail at the P.O. box would be directed to the club by the post office. However, the club, being a private organization, held information about its members in the strictest confidence, thus shielding them from any public inquiry.

It is interesting to note that any group that has an address that it is willing to have disclosed to the public can use that address to shield the addresses of all members of the group. It also seems that the USPS has no direct objection to this setup. Just be sure to keep your box fees paid in a timely manner and rent a large enough box so that the volume of incoming mail does not repeatedly exceed the capacity of the box you are using.

Finally, it pays to keep an eye on what the USPS is doing. Because the USPS does many things without the consent of the American people (when was the last time you got to vote on a postal rate hike?) and has a monopoly on first class mail, it is important to keep an eye on what it is doing. An organization that keeps an eye on what the USPS is up to and how its actions affect our rightful liberty is Postal Watch, Inc. (www.postalwatch.org). Postal Watch is a private organization and is not affiliated with the USPS or any other governmental organization.

Chapter 31

Have Your Name Removed from DMA Mailing and Telemarketing Lists

How often do you pick up the mail only to find that most of what you receive is "junk mail"? If you are like most of us, you receive more junk mail than mail that is actually of interest. Junk mail does not pose a direct threat to our privacy and security in and of itself. However, the fact that your name, address, and who knows what other personal information is being sold, rented, or given to these companies that send out the junk mail filling your mailbox should be of concern.

The question to ask yourself—and perhaps the companies with which you choose to conduct business—is, "What right does a company have to use my personal information in its marketing schemes without my consent?" If a company is going to make a profit by selling your personal information, it should at least have your permission to do so.

While I have said that junk mail does not pose a direct threat to our privacy and security in and of itself, there is in fact a very real threat from direct marketing (junk mail) and telemarketers. Many companies are using prison inmates to conduct telemarketing and screen responses to direct marketing. The November 15, 2001, edition of the *Abilene Reporter-News* and the November 23, 2001, edition of *The Austin Chronicle* reported that a Texas woman, April Jordan, has filed a lawsuit against Salt Lake City, Utah-based SandStar Family Entertainment for putting her family at risk by using felons to conduct telemarketing. According to the reports, Jordan's 14-year-old daughter answered the felon's telemarketing call to the Jordan home, and, as a result, this felon obtained the girl's name, home address, age, physical description, and other personal information. The felon then provided this information to another inmate, who sent a suggestive letter to this young girl!

The use of inmates to make telemarketing calls and process marketing information is not a rare or unique occurrence. Major corporations, such as AT&T and Honda, are reported to have used inmates for telemarketing and data-entry purposes, and TWA is reported to have used inmates to make airline reservations.

There is perhaps a place for employing inmates (the old cliché of inmates making license plates comes to mind); however, using felons to gather personal information about you and your family is clearly a problem. If inmates are going to be used to conduct telemarketing and process personal information, this fact should be disclosed prior to the contacted party's revealing any information. (Inmates should be required to disclose at the beginning of the conversation that they are incarcerated and the telemarketing call is part of the prison work program.)

Even if you never deal with telemarketers, there is still the potential of finding your personal information in the hands of convicted and incarcerated felons, since direct marketing lists are sold and rented among various businesses.

I believe that before a company may disclose personal information about its customers (and this includes name and address), it should have the express consent of said customers. For people who want to receive marketing offers in the mail and have their names and addresses sold to other companies, there should be an "opt-in" option (i.e., "Initial here if we may use your name and address for marketing purposes.") Unfortunately, this is not the case, and most companies just assume that once you conduct business with them your personal information is theirs to do with as they please.

While there is no "opt-in" option available (and there certainly should be), there is an "opt-out" option available. Because most reputable businesses that engage in direct marketing (sending junk mail) are members of the Direct Marketing Association (DMA), you can notify the DMA Mail Preference Service and the DMA Telephone Preference Service that you do not wish to receive direct marketing ads and calls from telemarketers, and they will add you to a database of names and addresses to be excluded from mailing and telemarketing lists.

Once you notify the DMA of your preference, it will take a few months before you will notice a reduction in junk mail, but opting out with the DMA really does help. Of course, the DMA can do nothing to limit junk mail from companies that do not subscribe to it, so this is not an all-inclusive way to get rid of junk mail. However, opting out with the DMA is a free service; all it takes is a few moments of your time and a couple of postage stamps. To have your name removed from member mailing and/or telemarketing lists, contact the DMA at the following addresses:

Mail Preference Service
Direct Marketing Association
P. O. Box 9008
Farmingdale, NY 11735

and

Telephone Preference Service
Direct Marketing Association
P. O. Box 9015
Farmingdale, NY 11735

You can also register online with the DMA at www.thedma.org. There is a $5 fee to register online, whereas registering by mail is free. The DMA also has a commercial e-mail opt-out section to help you reduce SPAM. Even if you have already registered with the DMA, it is worth visiting its Web site to keep an eye on what direct marketers are doing and to watch for other privacy options.

CHAPTER 32

Limit Junk Mail

As we have seen, registering with the DMA is an effective tactic for reducing the amount of junk mail we receive and damming the flood of telemarketing calls that disrupt the privacy and peaceful enjoyment of our homes. While this is certainly effective to a point, it unfortunately won't put a complete end to the widespread use of personal and private information to enhance corporate profits. Not every direct marketer subscribes to the DMA lists of people who object to the sale of their personal information and the disruption of their privacy by corporate America.

There are a number of companies that specialize in the collection and sale of marketing data and in direct marketing of various products and services. In addition to registering with DMA, it is worthwhile to contact these companies directly and require that they delete your personal information from their databases and marketing lists.

The following are the companies to which you should send an "opt-out" letter:

Acxiom
301 Industrial Blvd.
Conway, AR 72302

ADVO-Systems
Director of List Maintenance
239 West Service Road
Hartford, CT 06120-1280

American Family Publishers
P.O. Box 62000
Tampa, FL 33662

Haines Criss-Cross Directory
Director of Data Processing
8050 Freedom Ave. NW
North Canton, OH 44720

Info USA
416 S. Bell Ave.
Ames, IA 50010

MetroMail (now Experian)
901 W. Bond St.
Lincoln, NE 68521-9989

National Direct Marketing Service
892 Worchester Road
Wellsley, MA 02482

National Demographics and Lifestyles
List Order Services
1621 18th St., Suite 300
Denver, CO 80202
(They collect and distribute information provided by consumers on warranty cards.)

Publishers Clearing House
101 Channel Drive
Port Washington, NY 11050

Readers Digest
Readers Digest Road
Pleasantville, NY 10570

Valpak Direct Marketing Systems, Inc.
Cox Target Media
Corporate Headquarters
8605 Largo Lakes Drive
Largo, FL 33773

Chapter 33

Using the U.S. Postal Service Prohibitory Order to Fight Junk Mail

"We therefore categorically reject the argument that a vendor has a right under the Constitution or otherwise to send unwanted material into the home of another. If this prohibition operates to impede the flow of even valid ideas, the answer is that no one has a right to press even "good" ideas on an unwilling recipient. That we are often "captives" outside the sanctuary of the home and subject to objectionable speech and other sound does not mean we must be captives everywhere. The asserted right of a mailer, we repeat, stops at the outer boundary of every person's domain."

—Justice Warren E. Burger, for the majority, in *Rowan, dba American Book Service, et al. v. United States Post Office Department, et al.* 397 U.S. 728 (1970)

OK . . . but what about the junk mailers that simply ignore your requests to be removed from their marketing lists and continue to distribute your private information? One answer to this problem is a U.S. Postal Service Prohibitory Order.

The original intent of the Prohibitory Order was to stop pornographers from mass-mailing sexually oriented material. After all, not everyone wants to receive this type of material in the mail, and these "sleaze merchants" had no way of knowing whether Johnny Jones on their mailing list was 6 years old or 60.

The problem arose with trying to determine what was sexually oriented material and what was not. Some people may find the Fredrick's of Hollywood catalog offensive; others may find the Sears catalog offensive.

In 1970, a case was appealed from the U.S. District Court for the Central District of California to the U.S. Supreme Court. The case, *Rowan, dba American Book Service, et al. v. United States Post Office Department, et al* 397 U.S. 728, concerned itself with what material the post office could prohibit from being sent to an addressee. Part of the argument was that the post office has no right to censor the mail and determine what is and what is not sexually oriented material.

The court agreed with this argument, for certainly the postal service is not in a position to make any such determination. However, the court also found that an addressee does not need to accept everything sent to him through the mail and should not have to put up with repeated mailing of material he finds objectionable.

The Supreme Court stated in its decision of May 4, 1970, "The addressee has complete and unfettered discretion in electing whether or not he desires to receive further material from a particular sender. . . . An addressee may file an application for a prohibitory order to stop delivery of a 'dry goods catalog' if he so chooses."

Yes, the Supreme Court has ruled that if you find the Sears catalog objectionable you can file an order with the postal service to prohibit its delivery to your address! To file a prohibitory order against a junk mailer, you must have actually received mail that you find objectionable (remember, you make the sole decision as to what you do and do not find objectionable). Take this material and complete a Postal Service Form 1500—Application for Listing and/or Prohibitory Order. The PS Form 1500 is available from any major post office, or may be downloaded from the USPS Web site (www.usps.gov). Now take the material you wish to stop receiving (find objectionable) and the completed PS Form 1500 to any post office and turn it in.

You may find that if you actually attach a dry goods catalog (or other general junk mail) to the PS Form 1500 and turn it into your local post office, the postal clerk will refuse to accept it because in "his opinion" that material is not offensive. In this case you could try to explain the Supreme Court's ruling to him, but this may be more effort than it's worth. It may be better to point out Postal Bulletin 21977, 30 September 1998, p. 13, which states, "Postmasters may not refuse to accept a Form 1500 because the advertisement in question does not appear to be sexually oriented. Only the addressee may make that determination." If all else fails, simply send the completed form and associated objectionable material directly to the Prohibitory Order Processing Center (although you will end up paying the postage this way), at the following address:

Prohibitory Order Processing Center
U.S. Postal Service
Post Office Box 3744
Memphis, TN 38173-0744

Some may ask if it's really worth all this effort to have oneself removed from the various direct marketing databases and mailing lists. Personally, I believe it is worth the effort because it is one more step toward regaining personal privacy. Furthermore, there is not that much work involved in registering with the DMA and sending an opt-out letter to the companies listed above. Even if you end up filing a couple PS Forms 1500, it only takes a moment to do so (unless you have to explain matters to an uninformed postal clerk).

As with registering with the DMA, it will take a few months from the time you send opt-out letters to the companies listed here before everything is processed and you begin to see a marked reduction in junk mail, but it will happen.

Chapter 34

Double-Wrap Your Postal Mail

Surreptitious opening of most envelopes sent through the mail takes little effort and only minimal skill. Instructions are readily available on the Internet and in books such as *CIA Flaps and Seals Manual* (Paladin Press).

While your mail is in the hands of the postal service it is relatively secure from outside snooping but readily available to postal employees and the alphabet soup of government agencies that may, for whatever reason, take an interest in your private correspondence. If your mail is delivered to your home, perhaps to a box at the end of your driveway, someone can easily remove your mail before you do, unless you are waiting when the postman delivers it. If a private investigator or the neighborhood snoop removed private letters from your mailbox, carefully opened them, recorded the contents, and then resealed them and returned them to your mailbox, would you know it? If you received a letter in the mail on Wednesday instead of Tuesday, would you be aware that it had been missing for a day?

When government agencies send sensitive material, they double-wrap it to prevent its surreptitious opening. The government procedure is to place the sensitive material in an envelope, seal all seams and edges with tape, and record appropriate addresses and security markings on the envelope. This envelope is then placed into a second envelope, which then has all its edges and seams sealed with tape. The outer envelope is addressed, but there are no security markings recorded on it. This is effective, but the outer envelope with all edges and seams sealed with tape stands out from ordinary mail.

For security of personal correspondence I recommend double-wrapping your private letters, but with a bit of a change. Instead of sealing just the edges of the inner envelope, I use clear sealing tape or clear packing tape. Cut a length of tape twice the length of your inner envelope. Place the tape on a table, adhesive side up. You may need two strips of sealing/packing tape to cover the entire width of the envelope (I was able to obtain 4-inch-wide packing tape, which works well for the smaller 3 5/8 x 6-inch personal correspondence envelopes, from a local moving company). Now, after sealing your envelope, place it on the adhesive portion of the tape and then fold the tape around the envelope so that it covers all surfaces. Leave a slight edge of tape around the envelope so that you have an adhesive-to-adhesive seal. This type of seal, covering all surfaces of the envelope, is damn near impossible to get into in a surreptitious manner.

Now, place the sealed envelope in an outer envelope and seal and address it normally. The outer envelope doesn't stand out from other letters, but your private correspondence sealed inside is protected from snoops. Even the old trick of using chemical sprays to make the envelope momentarily transparent won't work because the inner envelope is completely wrapped in tape and therefore impenetrable by these sprays.

PART VI

COUNTERING THREATS TO HOME SECURITY AND PRIVACY

CHAPTER 35

Secure Your Home to Ensure Personal Privacy

When we think of physical security (restricting physical access to a place or thing), we may consider it a crime-prevention measure. The lock on your front door and the vault at the bank certainly help to keep burglars out, but physical security is also an essential element of personal privacy.

The security of our homes may in fact be one of the most essential elements of personal privacy. When we are in our own homes we should be shielded from outside influences, interruptions, and intrusions. What we do in the privacy of our homes should be nobody's concern but our own. Of course, I don't advocate the acceptance of ongoing criminal activity simply because someone chooses to conduct those activities in the privacy of his or her own home. There are things that are evil in and of themselves (*malum in se*)—things which, by their very nature, tread upon the rightful liberty of others. When this is the case, there may be justification for intervention by local or other law enforcement agencies. However, in most cases there can be no justification for anyone's interference with the private actions of individuals in their own homes. Unfortunately, the principle that a person's home is sacred is often ignored by those who have no regard for freedom.

There is a growing and alarming trend among investigators—ranging from Joe Sleaze, Private Eye, to rogue government agents—toward sneaking into private homes for the purpose of gathering information or evidence. When a private individual engages in such activity, it is certainly criminal. When Big Brother conducts business using such actions, it would still seem to violate the provisions of law and due process. Rule 41(d) of the Federal Rules of Criminal Procedure specifically states that a government agent executing a search warrant "shall leave a copy and receipt at the place from which the property was taken." Furthermore, the U.S. Supreme Court has traditionally held that, absent exigent circumstances, a government agent executing a search warrant must knock and announce himself (*Richardson v. Wisconsin*, 520 U.S. 385, 1997). This would seem to preclude the possibility of Big Brother's prying about our homes and offices on covert fishing expeditions.

Unfortunately, the FBI has been known to engage in such activity from time to time, although it would seem that they have no legal authority for their blatant disregard for the 4th Amendment rights of American citizens during these covert actions!

While we may want to believe that FBI covert operations are intended only to combat international terrorism and narcotics trafficking, this does not appear to be the case. Although current information about Big Brother's covert operations against American citizens remains shrouded in secrecy and the few cases that have come before the courts are fragmented and confused, we need only look back at recent history to see the results of government disregard for Constitutional freedoms.

From 1956 to 1971 the FBI ran program of covert activity against American citizens in the name of national security. This program was known as COINTELPRO and consisted of ongoing covert surveillance, harassment, and criminal activity directed against American citizens by government agents. Some insight into this illegal activity can be found in the following quote from the "Final Report of the Select Committee to Study Governmental Operations with Respect to Intelligence Activities of the United States Senate, 94th Congress, 2nd Session, 1976" (The Church Committee Report):

> COINTELPRO is the FBI acronym for a series of covert action programs directed against domestic groups. In these programs, the Bureau went beyond the collection of intelligence to secret action defined to "disrupt" and "neutralize" target groups and individuals. The techniques were adopted wholesale from wartime counterintelligence, and ranged from the trivial (mailing reprints of Reader's Digest articles to college administrators) to the degrading (sending anonymous poison-pen letters intended to break up marriages) and the dangerous (encouraging gang warfare and falsely labeling members of a violent group as police informers).

Now, we certainly want our law enforcement agencies to be able to conduct investigations. Such investigative work may well require surveillance and perhaps some types of covert operations undertaken to infiltrate criminal organizations. However, this activity must be conducted within very limited and defined boundaries and, most importantly, must jealously safeguard the constitutional rights and freedoms of those under investigation. I personally can't see how breaking up marriages and encouraging gang warfare in American cities qualify as legitimate law-enforcement functions.

The Church Committee Report is probably available from most major libraries, and it is available online along with other information about the FBI's COINTELPRO operations against American citizens. Before granting government agencies broad powers to influence the lives of American citizens, it is essential that we be aware of how they have used such power in the past—and what this portends for the future.

Unfortunately, federal agencies run amok are not the only problem we have to deal with (and perhaps not even the most likely problem). State and local government agencies have no better track record than our public servants in federal agencies when it comes to safeguarding the rightful liberty of the American people. We are also faced with the additional problem of private agencies and investigators who may, for a fee, take an interest in our activities. When Joe Sleaze, Private Eye, picks the lock on your front door and sneaks in to make a copy of the files on your home computer, he is breaking the law, but that doesn't mean that such things don't happen.

Covert investigative activity conducted against American citizens is nothing new. It is an ongoing activity undertaken by everyone from our public servants in federal agencies to private individuals with some interest in disrupting your life. It is therefore important to consider physical security as part of your countermeasures planning. If Joe Sleaze, Private Eye and Big Brother are unable to bypass the lock that restricts access to your computer, they won't be able to copy files from it.

Chapter 36

Place a Barrier between the Public Street and Your Front Door

The privacy and sanctity of one's home should be assured. Unfortunately, there are those who believe that their particular cause takes precedence over your peaceful enjoyment of your home. Jehovah's Witnesses, Mormons, Baptists, Girl Scouts selling cookies, students selling magazine subscriptions, some guy selling encyclopedias, or any number of other possible intruders can violate the privacy of your home. A sign stating "No Trespassing" or "No Soliciting" should be sufficient to keep you from being disturbed in polite society, but such signs are easily and frequently ignored by those going door to door.

Because of the prevalence of door-to-door solicitation in some communities, criminals seeking to "case your place" for some future action and investigators hoping for a quick look inside often use the guise of a solicitor. Furthermore, even "legitimate" solicitors may be difficult to get rid of until you agree to purchase whatever they are hawking or support the group they are advocating.

To keep unwanted company from knocking on your front door, it is necessary to place a barrier between the public street and your front door. This barrier does not need to be a 12-foot-tall electric fence, but rather anything that keeps people from easily approaching your home from the public street. A decorative fence around your yard combined with a locking gate will keep solicitors at bay.

Not everyone, however, has a yard around which to erect a fence. A gate blocking the steps onto your front porch can prove just as effective, as can a locked door at the main entrance of an apartment building. The idea is to make the approaching your front door more effort than it is worth for the solicitor, salesman, or snoop.

That said, the effectiveness of a dog in deterring solicitors, trespassers, and other door-to-door nuisances cannot be overlooked (although a dog does not have the same effect as a physical barrier). Of course, the effectiveness of a dog in discouraging people from approaching your door depends a great deal on the disposition of the dog. Almost any dog will bark at the approach of a stranger; however, a barking dog may not prevent someone from approaching your door unless it is clearly of a mind to do so. Many door-to-door solicitors are used to dealing with dogs and may simply ignore the dog's bark unless the dog appears ready to back the bark up with some bite.

This does not mean that your dog must be Cujo on steroids to deter solicitors, but it must give enough of an aggressive appearance that solicitors won't be willing to tempt fate and the dog's temperament for the sake of a sale.

Even if your dog happens to be Cerberus who could guard the gates of hell, there should still be a locked gate for him to guard. I strongly believe that dogs provide an excellent addition to your personal and home security, and their acute senses detect trespassers where people may not, but a dog is not a replacement for a physical barrier. Rather, he is an addition to it!

Chapter 37

Install a Home Alarm System

Every home, whether it is a multi-million-dollar mansion or the lowliest shack, should be protected by an alarm system. No matter what intrinsic value your home may have, it is where you spend much of your time and keep most of your personal possessions. An alarm system is an important step in protecting yourself and your personal possessions against intruders.

There are several different types of alarm systems available, ranging from portable alarms costing about $20 to systems starting at several thousand dollars for installation, followed by a monthly monitoring fee. To determine what type of alarm is right for you, let's look at just what an alarm should do.

If we look at a simple definition of the word "alarm," we see that it has several different meanings:

alarm (n.)—a signal for giving notice of an emergency, rousing from sleep, etc.

alarm (v.)—to make fearful or apprehensive.
alarm (n.)—a call to arms.

To be effective, a home alarm system must do all these things. It must sound a signal to warn of an emergency. It must cause fear and apprehension in any intruder, causing him to flee. And it must serve as a call to arms, triggering a response to the emergency at hand.

I generally do not favor alarm systems set up and monitored by some alarm company. They have their place, but for the average home they offer no great advantage. With a centrally monitored alarm system, your system is connected to a monitoring station via telephone lines. The monitoring station is not usually local, however, and may in fact be in another state completely.

When the alarm is tripped at your home, a signal is sent to the alarm monitoring station. Upon receiving the signal that your alarm has been triggered, a monitoring station attendant will make a telephone call to your home to confirm that this is not a false alarm (the alarm wasn't accidentally set off by you). If there is no answer, the attendant will then call the police (or other security response) to go to your home and investigate the alarm. If, on the other hand, someone answers your phone, the attendant will ask for your security code/password to confirm that the alarm was unintentional. If the person who answers your phone doesn't know the security code/password (or gives an incorrect one), the monitoring station calls the police to respond to the alarm.

When the police receive a call from the alarm monitoring station, do they send all available units rushing to your aid and put the SWAT team on alert? Absolutely not! In fact, while the call will certainly result in the police paying you a visit to check things out, it is unlikely that it will elicit any type of priority response at all. The sheer number of false alarms precludes the police from rushing to check out every such call. Remember, this isn't a homeowner calling the police saying, "I need help"; it's an alarm company saying there is an alarm at a given address.

If you are not going to use a centrally monitored alarm, you are left with the option of a local alarm system. I prefer a properly designed local system to a centrally monitored system in most cases. When you set up your alarm system, you are going to meet the three basic requirements of an alarm: generate an emergency signal, frighten away an intruder, and provide a call to arms.

The emergency signal, of course, is the alarm signal itself. When the alarm sounds, it warns you that something is amiss. It may be as simple as the smoke detector announcing that fact that you burnt your morning toast or the perimeter system indicating that you left the back door open. It may also indicate a true emergency, such as the fact that the kitchen is on fire or a burglar has broken through your back door at 2 A.M.

If a burglar has broken through the back door at 2 A.M., you want your alarm system to frighten him away. This means *very loud* alarms and bright lights. Most burglars are not planning to encounter alarms and will flee immediately if they trip one.

Yes, there are criminals who can bypass your alarm system—or simply ignore it while they do whatever it is they plan to do and then flee before any response to the alarm is likely. However, they are the exception rather than the rule, and even they will leave the area quickly once an alarm sounds. (After all, someone might show up more quickly than they expect.) Most thieves are amateurs and opportunists and do not come prepared to deal with alarms and other security devices.

The "call to arms" is where centrally monitored alarm systems claim an advantage, stating that the police or security company will always be sent to investigate the calls they generate. You can, however, accomplish the same thing with a local system by incorporating an automatic dialer into the system. An automatic dialer is simply a device that connects your alarm to your telephone. When the alarm is triggered, the automatic dialer calls a selected number (or numbers—most can be set to call more than one) and plays a prerecorded message.

I have the automatic dialer on my alarm system programmed to call my cellular telephone (which is always with me when I am out) and a couple of other numbers where people are likely to be available to receive the call and respond to an alarm. Like the centrally monitored alarm system, I can call the police once I receive a call warning me that my home alarm has been triggered if I choose to do so. But when I call the police, I am the homeowner calling and saying that I need help. I know that I did not accidentally set off the alarm. I can give the police much more detailed information than an alarm monitoring company in some other state can. Because of this, I am much more likely to get a priority police response.

When installing your own alarm system, you should begin by planning a defense in layers.

You start at the outer perimeter of your property. This may be the beginning of a private road leading to your home, the fence around your yard, or the exterior wall of your apartment. The idea here is to establish the outer perimeter of your alarm system at the greatest distance that you can control. If you have a long driveway, a sensor at the end of it signaling when someone starts to approach your home is an example of an outer perimeter sensor. So too is the switch that signals when someone opens the gate around your yard and the sensor that turns on lights at night as someone walks up the path to your front door. The outer perimeter sensors need not trigger the alarm itself; they should simply alert you to the fact that someone is at the perimeter of your property and is likely approaching your home.

Having covered the outer perimeter, you now move to the exterior walls of your home, or the inner perimeter. This is the same whether you live in a single-family home or a multi-family apartment building—you concern yourself with the actual entrances (doors and windows) into your home. The inner perimeter alarm system will cover all of your doors and windows. Normally, you will use magnetic switches on your doors and moveable windows. These switches are placed so that the circuit is complete when doors and windows are closed. When a door or window is opened, the circuit is broken and the alarm sounds. On windows you may also want to include glass-break detectors, which will sound the alarm if a window is broken instead of being opened. The inner perimeter alarm is used when you are away from home, but, more importantly, it is used when you are home and want to protect the perimeter of your home (such as when you are sleeping).

Finally, interior sensors (motion sensors) are used to detect any motion in your home when you are away. If no one is supposed to be in your home, there should be no motion. Interior sensors watch for and detect any unauthorized movement.

Even if you cannot afford a complete and complex alarm system, any type of alarm is better than none at all. Begin with whatever you can afford and build from there.

Chapter 38

Install High-Security Locks

We all have some type of lock on the doors to our homes and businesses. Unfortunately most locks are not designed to prevent surreptitious entry. The majority of locks we install in our homes and businesses are intended to restrict forced entry—that is, to hold a door in a closed position, preventing it from being opened and resisting some degree of force against the door and lock.

While most quality locks do a fair job of restricting forced entry, they do little to prevent surreptitious entry. It takes only limited skill and practice to be able to pick open the locks most commonly used to protect your home. It takes even less practice and only slightly more time for a determined thief or snoop to impression a key to these locks and thus have repeated access to the area protected by the lock.

Covert entry teams usually have a skilled locksmith ready to quickly bypass any lock the team may run into as it goes about its secret affairs. From a countermeasures standpoint, we need to defeat this locksmith. Fortunately, this is just a matter of installing high-security, "pick-proof" locks to protect our homes. Technically, there is perhaps no truly pickproof lock, since any lock can be bypassed under laboratory conditions given sufficient time. However, there are locks that are virtually pickproof under field conditions.

I personally use Medeco High Security locks throughout my home, thereby virtually eliminating the possibility of anyone's sneaking into my home by surreptitiously bypassing the locks. These locks are as pickproof as one can get.

When considering privacy and countermeasures, it pays to choose locks that cannot be bypassed surreptitiously. Just as important as defeating rogue government agents or Joe Sleaze, Private Eye, is ensuring that no third party maintains a key to your home.

If you live in an apartment or other rental property, it is very likely that the landlord has a key to gain access to your home. This is completely legal and may be part of your rental contract. Nevertheless, the landlord is not supposed to enter your home, except in an emergency, without giving you advanced notice. Too often, however, landlords enter the apartments of their renters without giving the required advanced notice.

If you live in an apartment or other rental property, change the locks! Keep the old locks so that you can put them back if you move out. Changing the locks my be a minor violation of your rental agreement, but if the landlord is providing you with the required advanced notice for entering your apartment, you can be there to let him in. If he is trying to enter your apartment without giving you notice, you should be asking why he was trying to sneak into your apartment in the first place. Changing the locks keeps all those who don't belong in your home out, snooping landlords included!

Chapter 39

Use a Lockbox for Your Emergency Key

If you have installed high-security locks on the entrances to your home it will be very difficult to bypass these locks without the proper key. This is as it should be, but what happens if you lose your keys, or end up locked out of your home some other way?

Many people hide an emergency key outside their homes to allow them to gain access if they have managed to lock themselves out. Every basic security book, Neighborhood Watch flier, and crime prevention bulletin advises against leaving a key under the doormat, hidden in the potted plant on your front porch, or otherwise hidden outside your home. I agree with this advice, but I also understand that many people are going to hide an "emergency key" outside their home regardless of any security advice they may receive.

If you are determined to do this, I recommend that you first obtain a Realtor's lockbox. A small safe on a hasp, the lockbox is used by Realtors to leave keys outside of the homes they are showing to various clients. Realtors place these lockboxes, with a key locked inside, on the doorknob or elsewhere near the front door of the properties they are showing. Only Realtors authorized to show the property know the combination to the lockbox in order to obtain the key.

If you use a lockbox to secure your emergency key, you will not want to attach it to your front door or some other location where it can be easily found. Instead, secure it out of sight in a location near your home. These lockboxes are very strong, and it would take considerable force to break one open. Any burglar willing to expend the effort to break open the lockbox could more easily break through a window or hammer down your front door to gain access to your home.

Of course, using a Realtor's lockbox to secure an emergency key means that you must remember the combination to the lockbox. But if you are going to leave a key to your home outside where it may be found, the small effort required to remember a combination is certainly worth it.

Part V

ENHANCING PRIVACY AND PERSONAL SECURITY: MISCELLANEOUS TIPS

Chapter 40

Use a Paper Shredder

Think for a moment about the things that you throw out in the trash. Now I don't mean baby's dirty diapers or that leftover slice of pizza from "Tommi's Pizza Emporium," but those things that give someone a detailed view of your personal life. Do you ever throw out credit card or bank statements? How about any of the following:

Address labels from mail and magazines
ATM receipts
Anything with your Social Security number
Documents containing your maiden name
Documents containing names, addresses, phone numbers, or e-mail addresses
Documents relating to investments
Documents containing passwords or PIN numbers
Documents containing your driver's license number

Employment records
Legal documents
Investment, stock, and property transactions
Items with your signature
Itemized grocery receipts
Luggage tags
Medical and dental records
Pay stubs
Personal letters
Preapproved credit card offers
Receipts with checking account numbers
Report cards
Resumés or curriculum vitae
Tax forms
Transcripts
Travel itineraries
Used airline tickets
Utility bills

If I can analyze your trash for a month, I can build a detailed profile about your life. So too can any private investigator, government agent, nosy neighbor, or stalker. If you ever read some of the books that teach techniques for harassment and revenge, they all point out that to disrupt someone's life you have to learn something about that person. These books often recommend going through a person's trash to learn information that can be used against him. To foil trash analysis, anything that might reveal information about your personal life should be shredded before being thrown out.

Paper shredders are available for just a few dollars from any office supply store. When you purchase a paper shredder, you will have the choice of buying a strip shredder or a crosscut shredder. The strip shredder will generally be slightly less expensive and will allow a higher volume of shredding (you can shred more pages at once with a strip shredder than you can with a crosscut shredder). The crosscut shredder offers a higher degree of security in that there is generally no hope of reassembling a document that has been run through a crosscut shredder.

So does this mean that someone can reassemble a document that has been run through a strip shredder? The lower-priced strip shredders generally shred a document into 1/4-inch continuous strips. Given a single document run through a shredder and a reasonable amount of time, it could be reassembled. Even with a few shredded documents, someone with sufficient motivation and time may be able to reassemble strip-shredded documents. This was demonstrated in the case of *United States v. Scott*, 975 F2d. 927, 1992 U.S. App., where IRS agents picked through the trash of a Massachusetts man and reassembled documents he had shredded, thereafter using those documents against him.

However, when dealing with strip shredders, you must take into account a concept known as "secure volume." Simply put, secure volume is shredding a great enough volume of like paper to preclude reassembling the documents. Regarding secure volume and the destruction of documents, government security regulations state,

> The "secure volume" concept of destruction processing stresses that security is enhanced not only by small residue particle size but also by restricting the chances of successful reconstruction of that residue by increasing the number of pieces involved. This increase can be achieved in two ways: prohibit destruction until a quantity of no less than 20 similar pages of classified paper are destroyed at one time, or add sufficient similar type of unclassified pages of paper to the classified

> document to arrive at the minimum 20 similar page count. Either method will result in a "secure volume" of residue. (Army Regulation 380-5, Appendix K2, paragraph a)

I tend to favor the crosscut shredder because it gives the greatest degree of security. I believe that the additional cost is well justified when you consider the security advantages. But if you are on a tight budget, by all means use a strip shredder and the secure volume method of shredding. Any type of shredding is preferable to placing intact documents in the trash. If you come up with a document that is particularly sensitive and you don't want to chance that it might be reassembled (no matter how slim that chance might be), burn it! No single destruction method has been found to be as effective, versatile, and secure as burning. However, burning any quantity of documents tends to be messy and may not be an option if you live in the middle of Los Angeles or a similar location with strict rules against burning trash. However, if it's a matter of destroying a few pages infrequently, burning is certainly an option, and everything else goes through your shredder.

CHAPTER 41

Establish an Alternate Identity

At one time or another we have all wished that we could be someone else. It's possible to make that wish come true by establishing an alternate identity. When you think of alternate identity (or fake ID), the first thing that probably comes to mind is teenagers with a fake driver's license trying to buy beer and cigarettes, or maybe a con man passing bad checks or some criminal on the run from the law. But while alternate identity can be used for criminal purposes, it can also serve to enhance your personal privacy and security.

Many celebrities work under "stage names," and authors may write under "pen names." Here are a few celebrities' names that you may not recognize, and their stage names, which you will probably recognize easily:

Marion Robert Morrison . . . . John Wayne
Norma Jeane Mortenson (later Baker) . . Marilyn Monroe
William Henry Pratt . . . . Boris Karloff
Ehrich Weiss . . . . Harry Houdini

Dianne Belmont . . . . Lucille Ball
Archibald Leach . . . . Cary Grant

Nobody would accuse these celebrities of being criminals because they used stage names (had alternate identities). We simply recognize that these individuals have a public life and a private life. But you don't have to be a celebrity to want to maintain some degree of privacy in your life, and establishing an alternate identity offers a way for anyone to do this.

Too often when building an alternate identity, people make the mistake of wanting to put the whole thing together in a week. Building an effective alternate identity will take several months before it has any real foundation or usefulness.

When planning an alternate identity, it is first necessary to work it out on paper. Name, date, place of birth, parents' names (and mother's maiden name), occupation, and so on are all important considerations. Where did this fictitious individual go to school? What jobs has he or she held? It's important to take the time to plan and write a life history that fits the new person being created—one that is comfortable and easy to remember.

Once a basic life history has been written, it must be examined with a critical eye to be sure that it meets the requirements of basic common sense and will not raise any flags because of unintentional errors. Let's look at a few pieces of the alternate identity.

Name: The name selected can't just be anything; it should be one that is fairly common, particularly to the area the new person is from (or is claiming to be from). For example, there are likely to be several pages of Johnsons listed in any local telephone book. On the other hand, there will probably only be one or two listings for the name Drzybylowicz, if any (depending on the city). No offense to any Drzybylowicz's reading this book, but for an alternate identity, the name must blend into the background. It should also be consistent with the heritage (or perceived ethnicity) of the new person being "created." There may be a few Olsens of Asian heritage, but there are probably many more Lees.

Age and Date of Birth: When choosing a birthday for one's new identity, the day and month can be almost anything; however, one should not stray too far from reality when selecting the year. A person who is 25 and looks 18 would not want to claim to be 50 when using his alternate identity. And using one's real birth date is not a good idea, since the date-of-birth field in databases can be and often is used for tracking purposes.

Place of Birth: Large metropolitan areas with lots of people and bureaucracy are excellent choices. There may have been 50 people named David Johnson born in New York City last year. A good alternate identity will easily blend into a crowd and get confused in the bureaucracy.

Parents and Family History: Just as a new person is developed for the alternate identity, so too are that person's parents and family. "Mother's maiden name" is a common question on applications and is often used to verify an individual's identity (particularly over the telephone), so being consistent with this fabrication is an essential part of building an alternate ID.

The next item needed to establish a new identity is a mailing address. This can be difficult or easy, depending on one's circumstances. Anyone who tries to secure either a post office box or a private box at a commercial mail-receiving agency such as Mail Boxes Etc. will be required to present two pieces of identification (one of which must be photo ID). It may, however, be possible to begin receiving mail in other ways. A person who lives in a large apartment complex (or has access to one) with mailboxes in a common area may be able to make use of an unused box to begin receiving mail.

In a rural area, it might be possible to mount a mailbox in line with others along a rural road. In many rural areas, mailboxes are found in clusters along a road or at the intersection of a couple of roads, and the actual homes are down long drives or private roads coming off the county road where the rural mail carrier delivers. When putting a rural mailbox in place, however, it's important to be sure that the house number used on the box does not actually exist. (If the last house number on a particular street is 824, it might be possible to add a box at the intersection using 828 or 833 as the house number. Since house numbers in rural areas tend to be a little disorganized, nobody will likely notice that there is no house associated with the new mailbox.

Once the new box is placed in line with others, the rural carrier will probably leave a PS Form 4232—Rural Customer Delivery Instructions. This form should be filled out using the alternate ID information and placed back in the box for the postal carrier, who will pick it up and file it for his route. There is no ID requirement here. It's now possible to begin receiving mail addressed to the name selected for the new identity at the new "street address." It's a good idea to send a test letter to see what happens. If the address works without raising any red flags, it can then be safely incorporated into the alternate identity.

A major advantage of using a mailbox associated with an apartment building or along a rural road is that this gives the appearance of a "street address" to anyone looking at the address.

Once a basic life history and address are established, the alternate identity can be brought to life. It might be used to subscribe to a magazine or two (paid for with a money order), register with the various "people finders" on the Internet, and set up an e-mail account or two (e.g., alternate-identity@hotmail.com). When building an alternate identity, one must take advantage of any and all opportunities to gather secondary and supporting identification. This includes things like "shopper preference cards" and membership in "buyers clubs." The idea is to do things that provide participants with ID cards without requiring them to present identification to begin with. For instance, one could join the National Rifle Association (NRA) or take a Red Cross CPR course under his alternate identity and thereby receive an NRA membership card and a Red Cross CPR card in his alternate name.

These are some good ways to establish secondary ID, but what about something a little more substantial? In this case we are talking about establishing "primary ID," which tends to mean, "government-issued photo ID" and an associated national identification number (SSN)?

First let's consider the SSN. Social Security numbers are legitimately used to administer one's Social Security account, and of course the IRS co-opted it for tax purposes. However, someone establishing an alternate identity is not going to be applying for Social Security, nor is he going to be filing taxes. But one's SSN is demanded on many forms where there is no need for it. In fact, this is true in the majority of cases. Although our government promised that the SSN would never become a national identification number, those promises turned out to be meaningless ("government promise" and "meaningless" are synonyms, after all). Normally, the most appropriate response to some bureaucrat's demand that you disclose personal information for which the bureaucrat has no legitimate use is to tell this clown to go to hell and just where he can stick his forms as he make the trip. However, someone who is building an alternate identity wants to appear to be just one more mindless sheep, bleating out whatever information is demanded.

In this case, he needs a number he can recite for these bureaucrats and fill in on various forms. He could just make up a number fitting the SSN format, but it's quite likely that in doing so he would choose a number that is the legitimate SSN of a real, living person—or, worse yet, one of the FBI's 10 Most Wanted, an IRS agent, or some other unsavory character! To avoid committing identity theft, intentionally defrauding someone, or attracting unwanted attention, he needs a number that will not be associated with another person. To this end, he can use what has become known as a "pocketbook SSN." There are several SSNs that have been included in advertising over the years. These were included on specimen Social Security cards placed in wallets and pocketbooks sold by various companies, or in some other form of advertising. For some reason—perhaps out of sheer stupidity or maybe as a form of protest against Big Brother's intrusion into our private lives—many people began using these pocketbook SSNs as their own. Thus, although these numbers have been used by many people, they are not legitimately assigned to anyone.

The Social Security Administration (SSA) list of the most common "pocketbook" or "specimen" SSNs that have been used by some organization for advertising includes the following:

022-28-1852 (Massachusetts)

141-18-6941 (Oklahoma)

212-09-7694 (Maryland)
042-10-3580 (Connecticut)
165-16-7999 (Pennsylvania)
219-09-9999 (Maryland)
062-36-0749 (New York)
165-18-7999 (Pennsylvania)
306-30-2348 (Indiana)
078-05-1120 (New York)
165-20-7999 (Pennsylvania)
308-12-5070 (Indiana)
095-07-3645 (New York)
165-22-7999 (Pennsylvania)
468-28-8779 (Minnesota)
128-03-6045 (New York)
165-24-7999 (Pennsylvania)
549-24-1889 (California)
135-01-6629 (New Jersey)
189-09-2294 (Pennsylvania)
987-65-4320 (No State)

More detailed lists can be found online from SSA archives at: http://policy.ssa.gov/poms.nsf/36f3b2ee954f0075852568c100630558/3c011b3a029ac16385256a51004de7ff?OpenDocument.

This is a bit much to type in by hand, so you can also use a search engine such as www.google.com and search the keywords "pocketbook ssn ssa.gov," which will bring up this link as the first listing.

For the purpose of developing an alternate identity, the place of birth should ideally match the SSN, so I have indicated which would be the issuing state for each of the pocketbook SSNs above.

By adopting one of the "pocketbook SSN" it is possible to add an SSN to one's alternate identity. The next step is to come up with that all-important photo ID. This is not as big a problem as one might think. All that's needed is a professional quality ID, not necessarily an ID actually issued by some government agency.

The reason for this is that people tend to believe what they see and generally have no way to confirm or cross-reference initial data with which they are presented. Look at it like this—suppose you ask me for ID and I hand you my New Hampshire driver's license. If we are not in New Hampshire and you are not from New Hampshire, you probably have no idea what an actual New Hampshire driver's license looks like anyway. However, when I hand you a professional quality document that has the format of a driver's license (photo, date of birth, driver's license number, etc.) you will likely accept it as valid government ID. If you could run this license through some database of valid driver's licenses or call the Department of Motor Vehicles in New Hampshire, you could possibly determine that it is a fake, but as I said before most ID checks are based on what's initially presented. There is seldom any attempt to validate the authenticity of the ID itself.

It is interesting to note that even government bureaucrats tend to believe what they see and accept as valid that which is presented unless they suspect fraud. So in most cases they will not even bat an eyelash as long as the person presenting the ID appears to be just one more mindless sheep complying with some government regulation and demand for personal information, and not someone who is trying to obtain some government benefit.

So how do people get that initial photo ID? They either buy it or make it. There are some excellent books available showing step-by-step instructions on how to construct alternate ID, so I won't rehash that here (Paladin Press devotes an entire section of its catalog to "New ID & Personal Freedom"). Anyone with a computer, scanner, digital camera, and good quality printer can be in the ID business. It just entails a bit of desktop publishing. When constructing ID and other "official" documents, it is important to use good quality material. A perfect ID printed on notebook paper won't pass the most cursory exam.

For those with more money than skill, it is also possible to purchase realistic looking "novelty ID" from various sources by simply searching the Internet for "Novelty ID" and/or "Fake ID." With these sites the quality tends to be reflected in the cost of the ID, but it's also possible to spend $100+ and get something that isn't very useful. Making any ID that may be needed is ideal, since it offers more control over all aspects of the ID and the ability to make changes and improvements as necessary. However, if the necessary desktop publishing setup is not available, purchasing the initial photo ID is the only option.

One advantage of building an alternate identity over the course of several months is that it begins to take on a life of its own as a result of aggressive marketing by various companies.

While writing this book I had the opportunity to see a segment from one of the many daily talk shows (*Sally Jesse Raphael*, 12/14/ 01). The topic of discussion was how a 3-year-old girl received a pre-approved credit card application. Her mother filled out the application giving the little girl's actual birthday (showing she was only 3), and even wrote in place of the signature something like, "I am only 3 and would like to buy a lot of toys, but my Mommy says no." One might think that this would be the end of this credit card pre-approval, but the little girl was actually issued a credit card! The credit card company only caught on when it received inquiries from the media after the little girl's mother made them aware of her daughter's increasing credit status.

This same type of preapproved status can easily happen with any alternate identity. More importantly, however, is that once the foundation of the alternate identity is in place, it's a simple matter to begin taking advantage of opportunities as they arise. As an example of this, many department store chains like to encourage customers to get a store charge card. They offer a free pen set (or some such thing) and 10 percent off today's purchase to anyone willing to take a minute and fill out their store charge card application. The applicant will usually receive the store charge card in the mail within a couple of weeks. As long as the application appears to be filled out properly and raises no red flags with the store's internal credit department, the credit card is issued almost as a matter of course. Department stores usually don't run outside credit checks on these applications. They know that issuing a few thousand low-limit store charge cards will encourage more shoppers to make purchases in their store. Of course, they may issue a card to a poor credit risk or two, but the number of people who get the card, make purchases in the store (and probably pay interest on those purchases over a few months) more than makes up for the few who may skip out on their $300 maximum balance.

Once some limited credit has been established with an alternate identity, the next step is to make use of it in order to begin building a credit history. Because small accounts that are handled responsibly lead to large accounts, it's critical that payments are made on time and that there is no unusual activity that might draw attention to the account. With a couple of store credit cards and a photo ID, it is easy to establish a checking account at a bank. Of course, any interest earned on that account will be reported to the IRS; however, there is nothing to report on an account that doesn't earn interest. Many banks offer a simple, no-fee, non-interest-bearing checking account. Some banks even allow customers to open accounts through the mail!

Of course, when one is establishing credit and maintaining accounts under an alternate identity, it is absolutely essential that any debts are paid promptly and accounts are handled responsibly! As long as debts are paid and accounts show a good credit history, any slight irregularity that might otherwise raise a red flag will probably be dismissed as irrelevant.

Building an alternate identity takes some effort, but it can also be fun to watch this "new person" develop from what was merely notes on paper several weeks before. Establishing the basic foundation of an alternate identity allows one to seize those opportunities that present themselves to build the identity over the months and years by adding additional and more official pieces to it.

Think about the times you have done something under your true identity that could have just as easily been done under an alternate identity—those times when you were asked for photo ID, only to have the clerk only halfway glance at what you presented. Such routine demands for photo ID could easily have been met with the most rudimentary "fake ID." Had this resulted in some additional ID being issued, an account being established, or a service being provided to you, it could have just as easily been issued, established, or provided to your alternate identity.

So suppose you were to create an alternate identity and someone were to discover some irregularity and confront you with it? First off, don't panic and launch into some long, drawn-out explanation. A simple reply such as, "I don't know; must be some computer glitch" will often suffice. An additional piece of alternate ID will often allay suspicion. And if someone seems ready to make too much out of some small irregularity, simply walk away. You can always abandon the whole ID and create another. (Of course, there is really nothing to prevent you from having more than one alternate identity at the same time.)

I have never had a problem using an alternate identity and getting others to accept it on face value once it has been in place for a few months. (I mean hypothetically, of course . . . I don't have any alternate identities.) When you are building alternate identity to give a degree of privacy and security to your true identity, there is little reason for anyone to question it in the first place. You are not skipping out on past debts, running out on parental responsibilities, or any other thing likely to bring close scrutiny on yourself. Rather, you use alternate identity to ensure that someone attempting to look at your true identity has nothing to find.

Chapter 42

Employ Antisurveillance Techniques

Surveillance is defined as the process of keeping a person under observation to get detailed information about his activities, operations, identity, and contacts with others. During a "discreet surveillance," it is intended that the subject of the surveillance (you) remain unaware that he is being followed and observed.

Surveillance is conducted by various government agents and law enforcement types, private investigators, stalkers, jealous spouses, terrorists, and various other unsavory elements of society. Therefore, antisurveillance, or the ability to detect surveillance and employ countermeasures to make it ineffective, can be an important skill.

Surveillance can be divided into two broad categories: fixed surveillance and moving surveillance. During a fixed surveillance, the surveillant (the person conducting the surveillance) remains in a fixed position. During a moving surveillance, the surveillant, or more likely a team of surveillants, follows you from place, observing your ongoing activity.

If you find yourself under surveillance, you will either be facing amateurs (those with little or no training in surveillance) or professionals (trained surveillance teams). Defeating amateur surveillants (and this includes various agencies and agents who may want to follow you around but are not specifically trained to conduct discreet surveillance) is not a particularly difficult problem. Defeating a professional surveillance team can be a major nightmare. The silver lining in this dark cloud, however, is that you will almost always be dealing with amateurs (at least initially).

First let's look at the fixed surveillance and what we can do about it. In this case the surveillants remain in a fixed and often concealed location while observing another static location. As an example, if someone takes a position to observe your home and records the times you come and go and the activity around your home but does not follow you when you leave, he is conducting a fixed surveillance. Over a period of time this would build a profile of your home life: What time do you get up in the morning? What time do you get home at night? What time do you go to bed? Do you have visitors on a regular basis?

A fixed surveillance can be difficult to detect because, assuming that the surveillants are well concealed (or at least don't seem out of place), there are no indicators of surveillance to detect.

To effectively counter a fixed surveillance you must begin by determining those areas from which a person could observe your home undetected. This can best be accomplished by getting out and viewing your house from any place that a surveillant might use. What can be seen from a vehicle in the parking lot down the street? What can be seen from that group of trees on the hill, or from the top floor of an office building three blocks away? As you become aware of the areas that could be used for a fixed surveillance, you will also become aware of people occupying those areas or attuned to changes to the areas that indicate that someone has recently been there.

When learning what can be observed from a fixed surveillance point, you will also learn what cannot be observed. This is important because you may find that you have the ability to come and go while remaining unobserved.

By its very nature a fixed surveillance is difficult to detect. Because of this, a progressive fixed surveillance may be used to gather information about someone who his very alert to the possibility of surveillance. In a progressive fixed surveillance the surveillants take up a position to observe you at a confirmed location (your home or work). When you leave, the fixed surveillance observes you as far as possible without changing location. The next day a fixed surveillance is established at the point where you became unobservable, and the process is repeated until a complete route of travel can be determined for you. A progressive fixed surveillance is time-consuming but has the major advantage of being nearly impossible to detect (as long as the surveillants remain concealed).

From the countermeasures point of view, however, a progressive fixed surveillance is easy to defeat by constantly altering routes of travel and times of departure and arrival. A progressive fixed surveillance is used to learn the activity patterns of someone who would probably detect a moving surveillance (i.e., counterintelligence agents).

A moving surveillance is much easier to detect than a fixed surveillance. In this case the surveillants are following you as you go from place to place. They must go where you go and do what you do in order to observe your activities throughout the day. However, here you have an advantage in that you initiate all action and movement. Those conducting the surveillance must react and respond to your movements.

Because surveillants must key their actions to your activities, you can use a concept called TSDD (Time, Speed, Distance, Direction) to detect them. Activity has a general pattern to it that is measured with TSDD. If you alter any of these factors, thus causing a surveillant to alter any of these factors, you can detect him.

Time—This refers to the amount of time you spend in a given location or the amount of time spent doing a certain thing. Not too many people spend hours lingering over a meal in a fast-food restaurant. Likewise, people do not go to a movie and leave halfway through it (assuming, of course, that it isn't a Spike Lee film). By altering "normal" timing in our activities, we force surveillants to do the same and thus reveal themselves.

Speed—How quickly do you move from one place to another? Look at a busy sidewalk and notice the speed at which everyone moves along. There is a definite pace and pattern here. Someone moving faster or slower than this pace and pattern will stand out.

Distance—This is the space between one point and the next. If you observe someone in a store at a shopping mall and later observe the same person at a different store in the same shopping mall, this is not necessarily an indicator of surveillance. The distance is small and there is some likelihood that you and another person would end up in these two stores at the same time merely by coincidence. However, if you see this same person at a restaurant on the other side of town that same day, this is an indicator of surveillance. The likelihood of your moving from one location over a large distance to another location and having someone else make this same movement decreases as the distance increases (unless, of course, that person is keying on your activities).

Direction—People naturally move via the shortest route between two points as long as there is nothing along that route to obstruct their movement. This can be seen where people wear a path across a lawn instead of following a paved walkway. By altering this natural pattern of direction, you make it necessary for a surveillant to do the same thing (assuming he wants to continue to observe you) and in doing so are able to detect the person(s) following you.

By being observant of the TSDD factors, you will be able to detect surveillance. It is important, however, to avoid doing those things that are obviously intended to disrupt surveillance. Boarding a bus and jumping off just as it is ready to leave will probably cause the surveillant who boarded the bus with you to end up on a useless ride to the next stop, but it will not enable you to lose the surveillants that remained at the bus stop, preparing to follow the bus in another vehicle. It also lets all of the surveillants following you know that you are aware of the surveillance. Thereafter, they will just take additional precautions to avoid detection, or you will end up dealing with a professional surveillance team that you cannot detect.

As you employ antisurveillance techniques, they must appear to be (and must in fact become) a normal part of your daily activities. You must also learn to be aware of your surroundings. Pay attention to things that are out of place. As hard as a surveillance team will try to blend into an area, they don't really belong there. There will always be things that will reveal their presence. The trick is to be sufficiently aware of your surroundings to detect these clues.

The first and most important antisurveillance technique you can employ is to randomly vary your routes of travel. This will prevent a surveillance team from being able to establish fixed surveillance points along a known route in order to report your passage and activity along that route. This countermeasure foils the *direction* factor of TSDD. The surveillance team is unable to predict your direction of travel and thus must be prepared to cover multiple directions. This forces the team to place more people on the ground and gives you a greater chance of detecting some of them. Since a progressive fixed surveillance will not work if you vary your routes of travel regularly, it will force a surveillance team to use a moving surveillance in order to keep track of you.

In addition to varying routes of travel, you should make a point of varying your times of departure and arrival. If you leave your house every morning a 7 A.M., a surveillance team knows that they can acquire you at your home by arriving a few minutes before 7 A.M. and remaining in the area until you leave the house (at which time they can begin the day's surveillance of your activities). Even if you depart a little early or are running a little late sometimes, a surveillance team knows it needs to be in the area from, say, 6:45 A.M. to 7:15 A.M. to pick you up. However, if you can vary your departure time by 30 minutes each way, leaving each day sometime between 6:30 A.M. and 7:30 A.M., you force the surveillance team to be in place from at least 6:15 to 7:45 A.M. to determine whether you are making your usual morning departure and whether to begin their surveillance. This impacts the *time* factor of TSDD. It also forces the surveillance team to remain in the vicinity of your house for a significant length of time, making them easier to detect.

Varying the time of your departure also allows you to vary your *speed*. If you depart 30 minutes earlier than necessary to reach your destination in time, slow your speed to burn up some of this time. Because you also alter your routes of travel, a surveillance team will have to hang back and follow you. This makes them easier to detect. To see this technique in action, try driving five miles per hour slower than the posted speed limit on your local interstate highway. Everyone will pass you. Any vehicle that doesn't will stand out and be quickly identified.

The *distance* factor of TSDD can be the most difficult to apply as an antisurveillance technique, but when employed it works quite well. A surveillant planning to follow you to see whom you meet at lunch will be hard-pressed to maintain the surveillance if you drive to the airport and board a plane to Paris. Along this same line, if you drive to the other side of the state when the surveillance team assumed you were just stepping out for lunch, the team will often break off surveillance. The distance factor also helps you identify surveillants. When the blue van that you saw parked across the street from your office suddenly appears behind you in another state, it is certainly a clue that you are being followed!

You can also plan and employ antisurveillance routes (ASR), which are specifically designed to defeat surveillance. Unlike what you may see on television, this does not mean high-speed chases through the city streets and driving the wrong way down one-way streets. An ASR should appear to be a normal action yet cause surveillants to become channeled and trapped or dispersed and confused. As an example of an ASR, you may find that it is possible to leave a main route of travel and cut through a residential area. Many residential areas are full of one-way streets and cul-de-sacs yet are easy enough to slip through quickly for one familiar with the area. By slipping quickly into and out of an area like this you may cause a surveillance team to become confused in the maze of residential streets.

You can employ the same techniques on foot by quickly entering a building with multiple entrances and exits and leaving by a door not visible from the point where you entered. In order to watch for your exit, the surveillance team will attempt to quickly box (surround) the building that you entered, but by moving quickly in and out of the building you will usually beat the box. When employing this technique it is important to watch the people who enter the building at the same time you do and note whether any of them are around as you exit. The person who entered with you and watches you leave is a surveillant. The idea, however, is to move deliberately enough so that the person following you into the building misses your exit.

When planning an ASR, you may be able to use access to restricted locations to your advantage. Now, I don't mean that you are the Director of Alien Research at Area 51 (then again maybe you are)! However, if you have access to an underground parking garage that requires an access code to gain entrance, a surveillant will not be able to follow you into the parking garage without knowing the code. Most parking structures also have several pedestrian exits . . . so just act quickly and beat the box. Are you a member of the National Guard or did you retire from the military? You can enter a military base by showing your ID to the guards at the gate. Joe Sleaze, Private Eye, may not have access to the base and will be unable to follow you in. Are there government office buildings or an airport in your area? Make sure you are not carrying any metal and enter the areas that require you to pass through a metal detector. A surveillant will be stalled at the metal detector, particularly if he is part of a team and is carrying radio equipment for communication with the other team members. It may be that you have no access to restricted areas, but if you do, make use of these areas for your ASR.

The overall concept with antisurveillance techniques is to apply the principle of TSDD in order to detect surveillance and counter it. Let's look at an example of applying TSDD that I have personally used to defeat a surveillance team. While working in Europe I discovered that I was under surveillance by a professional surveillance team. At that time it was my habit to drive to a park near the city and get my morning exercise jogging in the park. The surveillance team followed me to the park and even employed a foot team to act as joggers and follow my route through the park.

In order to defeat this surveillance team, I employed the *speed* factor of TSDD. Arriving at the park in the morning dressed for jogging as usual, I parked my vehicle, walked to the back of my car, opened the trunk, unloaded my bicycle, and rode away. Vehicles couldn't follow in the park, and joggers couldn't keep up with a bicycle. Of course, the next time I went jogging in the park the surveillance team had their own bicycle, but this story serves as a good example of how natural actions can be incorporated into ASR in order to defeat surveillance.

To defeat surveillance it is essential that you remain aware of your surroundings. You won't be able to detect when something is out of place if you don't know what is normal for the area you are in. As you observe the area and people around you, keep the TSDD factors in mind. Just because someone seems to be employing one of the TSDD factors does not necessarily mean that you are under surveillance (although you could be). The basic principle I work with regarding TSDD is: *Once is happenstance, twice may be a coincidence, but the third time is always enemy action*. Finally, become very familiar with your neighborhood. Plan and incorporate ASR into your daily activities and you will make it nearly impossible for any amateur to conduct a surveillance of your activities.

You will also make it very difficult for a professional surveillance team to conduct a surveillance of your activities.

An important thing to remember with antisurveillance techniques is that they must be employed regularly and become a part of your daily activities. This makes any attempt to establish a baseline for you (to learn your routine habits and activities) extremely difficult and time-consuming.

Chapter 43

Cover Your Tracks: How to Disappear

If you make a point of employing the various countermeasures discussed throughout this book, you will succeed in becoming pretty much invisible to the world around you. However, your situation may call for even more drastic measures. It may be that you are reading this book because you literally need to disappear in order to get away from the constant intrusions into your private life that are commonplace these days. Perhaps you are seeking to escape a relationship gone bad or flee the attentions of a stalker. Whatever your reason for dropping out of sight and keeping a low profile, there are a few important considerations that will help you avoid being tracked to your new life and location.

The first thing you must realize is that making this break will require that you move to a new residence and obtain new employment. Any stalker, former lover, or fatal attraction from which you may be trying to escape likely knows your home and workplace. At a minimum, you will have to find a new residence and make every effort to ensure that it never becomes associated with your real name.

Before you make this move, it will be necessary to prepare. It is paramount that your new residence is in no way connected with your old residence. If there is a trail from your past life to your new, any competent investigator will find it. In preparation for your move, there are a couple things you should do to help conceal your new location from anyone trying to locate you:

- Establish a P.O. box at your old address and have all your mail sent there if it is currently being delivered to your home.
- Open a bank account in another state (but not in the state where you are planning to move). This can be done using your current address. Many banks will allow you to open an account through the mail.

You will now make a move to an intermediate address. This helps shield your transition from your old address to your new one. Ideally, this intermediate address is not traceable to you. I know of a lady fleeing a relationship gone bad who rented a small cabin at a campground during the "off-season." She paid the rent in cash, and there were no utilities, telephone, or other services established in her name while she was there. The only record that might have existed was information she provided when renting the cabin, all of which pointed back to the address she had abandoned. Sharing an apartment with a roommate where you split the rent and living expenses but everything is listed in the roommate's name is another good option.

The intermediate address is very important. Since most people don't make this type of move more than once or twice, it is not something with which you are likely to have any practical experience. The most important thing to keep in mind here is that anything you do that requires you to provide your name and address must point to your old address (the one you are abandoning). This way, when you leave the intermediate address there are no tracks to follow to your new residence. Any mistakes that leave a trail to where you went will only point to the intermediate address, and everything there will point back to your old address.

The intermediate address also adds a time factor between your old address and your new one. When attempting to track down a person who has gone missing, an investigator will first look for clues as to where the person may have gone, and then he will look for clues to that person's exact whereabouts at the new location. If those clues are scarce, he will typically set the investigation aside for a month or so in order to give the missing person time to settle into his new life and start to leave clues that the investigator can use to locate him. These clues include things like telephone and utility accounts, children's school records, pet registration, vehicle registration, club memberships, subscriptions, and so on. The intermediate address (particularly if you are able to live with a roommate or in some other situation where you can avoid creating such records) prevents these common clues to your location from appearing when an investigator takes up the hunt after a month.

Ideally, while taking advantage of the time factor provided by the intermediate address, you are able to work and carefully plan for the move to your new home. When you make your actual move, DO NOT tell anyone your new address. Keep it a secret! Your actual residence must be shielded from disclosure in any type of record.

Your closest friends and family will of course know where you live if they are in a position to actually come visit you in your new home. However, those who are not in a position to visit you (perhaps they live on the other side of the country) do not need to have your physical address; just provide them with a mailing address.

There is very little need for anyone whom you do not plan to invite into your home to know where you actually live. As you go about your daily life, you will often find that there is this or that demand for your "street address," but as long as you provide something to fill in the blocks, your "mailing address" will almost always suffice.

Ask yourself, why does your bank need your "street address"? If you overdraw your account, is the banker going to stop by some afternoon to help you balance your checkbook? Of course not—the bank will simply refuse to pay any checks for which you have insufficient funds and send a notice of this deficiency to your mailing address. What about the local library or video rental store? If your library books are overdue or you are late returning a rented video, is someone going to pick these things up from you at your home and return them for you? You couldn't get them to come pick up the books or video even if you asked them to do so. What about the post office? If you rent a P.O. box they will demand that you disclose your "street address" (and provide two forms of ID), but there is no real reason for that information to be on file at the post office. Mail addressed to you will be placed in your P.O. box or held at the counter, but if you can't make it in to the post office to pick up your mail the postman isn't going to bring it by your home.

You will find that in almost all cases where there is some requirement that you disclose your street address there is no real need for that information. You can always argue the necessity of disclosing your street address, but that tends to overwhelm the mental capacity of that bureaucratic drone who can't see beyond the end of his form. In most cases it's just as easy to provide a meaningless, dead-end street address along with a mailing address to receive whatever correspondence may be necessary with regard to the matter at hand. When choosing this dead-end street address, it is important not to choose one that is actually someplace to which the post office can deliver. This prevents correspondence intended for you from being delivered to someone else if mail is inadvertently sent to your street address as opposed to your mailing address. You can develop a dead-end address by choosing a large apartment building with several different apartments (the more the better). Use the "street address" of the apartment building as your dead-end street address, but don't include any apartment number. Because there is no apartment number included in the address, the mail will be undeliverable and returned to sender. In a more rural setting, simply pick an area with a number of homes where mail is delivered to a group of mailboxes at the end of the street. Determine the highest house number in the area and pick one that's a couple of numbers higher for your dead-end street address. For example, if the last house number in the area is 447 Rural Drive, your address becomes 449 Rural Drive. There is no such address, but again, the "street address" requirement on most forms serves no purpose anyway. If there is ever any question regarding your nonexistent street address it will likely be written off to some kind of administrative error, especially since you are receiving mail at your P.O. box without any problem. (It is interesting to note that if the rural postal carrier delivers mail to boxes clustered at the end of the road, as opposed to delivering it to each physical house, you can add a new box to the cluster of mailboxes and actually receive mail there.)

OK . . . you are finally at your new address. You have covered your tracks and have made a clean break with your past. It is now essential that you employ a systematic pattern of countermeasures, as outlined throughout this book, to protect your privacy and rightful liberty.

Part VI

COUNTERING THREATS TO PERSONAL FREEDOM AND ACHIEVING SOVEREIGNTY

Chapter 44

Use NORFED American Liberty Dollars

NORFED (www.norfed.org) is the National Organization for the Repeal of the Federal Reserve Act and the Internal Revenue Code. NORFED points out the following:

> When congress unlawfully gave private interests the control of federal money, the sovereign States were left without any lawful money to use. By default, the people had to begin using Federal Reserve Bank Notes in lieu of gold or silver-backed currency. Originally the people's money was issued without interest and left little room for inflation. Today, however, Federal fiat money is loaned into circulation with interest and creates inflation.

NORFED issues American Liberty Dollars, which are warehouse receipts for a specific weight of pure .9999 fine gold or .999 fine silver that is stored in a warehouse in accordance with the Uniform Commercial Code (UCC).

Many of us are old enough to remember when our currency was actually backed by gold and silver. If you have coins issued prior to 1964, they were actually made of silver, having monetary value because of the silver content of the coin itself. Today gold and silver no longer back our currency, and our coins are made from base metals with no intrinsic value. NORFED's American Liberty Dollars give us the option of having a currency that is 100-percent backed by gold and silver—currency that is actually redeemable in gold and silver at NORFED redemption centers in 49 of these 50 United States.

If you were to look at an old $1 bill (silver certificate) issued by the U.S. government, you would find these words: "THIS CERTIFIES THAT THERE HAS BEEN DEPOSITED IN THE TREASURY OF THE UNITED STATES OF AMERICA ONE SILVER DOLLAR PAYABLE TO THE BEARER ON DEMAND." On the old $5 bill (silver certificate), you would find: "THIS CERTIFIES THAT THERE IS ON DEPOSIT IN THE TREASURY OF THE UNITED STATES OF AMERICA FIVE DOLLARS IN SILVER PAYABLE TO THE BEARER ON DEMAND." However, even if you were to take one of these old silver certificates and present it at your local bank (or even at one of the Federal Reserve Banks) demanding payment in silver as promised, you would not get it. Quite simply, the government maintains no gold and silver with which to pay these demands. Another government promise reduced to nothing more than empty and meaningless words!

On the other hand, NORFED's American Liberty Dollars are redeemable in gold and sliver, and NORFED minted coins are made of silver, thus having their own intrinsic value.

It is important to remember however that American Liberty Dollars are *not* an investment in gold and silver; rather, they are a currency. However, you will find that converting your federal reserve notes into American Liberty Dollars costs about the same as purchasing silver medallions and ingots from a dealer.

So, you ask . . . if American Liberty Dollars are a currency, what can I buy with them? The answer is pretty much anything you can buy using federal reserve notes. Of course, the business or individual from whom you wish to make a purchase must be willing to accept American Liberty Dollars, but there is an ever growing number of businesses and individuals that will do so. The NORFED Web site lists businesses in every state that accept American Liberty Dollars. Because American Liberty Dollars are a currency, you will often find that there is a cost difference when paying in American Liberty Dollars versus federal reserve notes. I have found that there are times when I can actually save money by making a purchase with American Liberty Dollars as opposed to federal reserve notes.

American Liberty Dollars are not (yet) a complete replacement for federal reserve notes, but they are a step in the right direction. If you own a business or provide a product or service, consider accepting American Liberty Dollars. By doing so, you make a stand for individual freedom and rightful liberty, while at the same time using a currency that has true value because it is 100-percent backed by gold and silver!

Chapter 45

Resist Government Trampling of Your Right to Travel Freely

The vast majority of us travel by automobile on an almost daily basis. We drive between home and work. We use our automobiles when we go shopping and when we go out to enjoy an evening's entertainment.

Unfortunately, travel by automobile is highly regulated and controlled by Big Brother. If you are going to drive an automobile on the public highways, every state requires that you obtain a state-issued permit, a "driver's license," to do so. Furthermore, the vehicle itself must be licensed and registered (license plates and registration sticker).

It may be rightly argued that travel on the public highways for private, as opposed to commercial, purposes is an exercise of our personal liberty:

> Personal liberty consists largely of the Right of locomotion—to go where and when one pleases—only so far restrained as the Rights of others may make it necessary for the welfare of all other

> citizens. The Right of the Citizen to travel upon the public highways and to transport his property thereon, by horsedrawn carriage, wagon, or automobile, is not a mere privilege which may be permitted or prohibited at will, but the common Right which he has under his Right to life, liberty, and the pursuit of happiness. Under this Constitutional guarantee one may, therefore, under normal conditions, travel at his inclination along the public highways or in public places, and while conducting himself in an orderly and decent manner, neither interfering with nor disturbing another's Rights, he will be protected, not only in his person, but in his safe conduct.
>
> —II *Am.Jur.* (1st) Constitutional Law, Sect. 329, p. 1135

Furthermore, personal liberty—the freedom to go where and when one pleases—is an inalienable right, not something to be licensed or restricted by Big Brother:

> Personal liberty, or the Right to enjoyment of life and liberty, is one of the fundamental or natural Rights, which has been protected by its inclusion as a guarantee in the various constitutions, which is not derived from, or dependent on, the U.S. Constitution, which may not be submitted to a vote and may not depend on the outcome of an election. It is one of the most sacred and valuable Rights, as sacred as the Right to private property . . . and is regarded as inalienable.
>
> —16 C.J.S., Constitutional Law, Sect. 202, p. 987

Unfortunately, it is the policy of every state that we surrender our Constitutional right of liberty for the state-granted and licensed privilege of traveling on the public highways. There is a maxim of law which states, "No public policy of a state can be allowed to override the positive guarantees of the U.S. Constitution." – (16 *Am.Jur.* (2nd), Constitutional Law, Sect. 70). Yet every state makes it a crime for the individual to travel upon the public highways, exercising his rightful liberty, without first obtaining written permission from Big Brother to do so!

The right to personal liberty (i.e., the right to travel upon the public highways) does not in any way absolve an individual of the requirement to operate his vehicle in a safe manner and to have a minimum degree of proficiency in operation of said vehicle. Some will argue that this is in fact the purpose of the driver's license—to ensure that everyone has acquired at least that minimum degree of proficiency in operating a vehicle. Were this actually the case, one might have little argument with the concept of driver's licenses, but the fact of the matter is that the driver's license is little better than a national ID card issued on a state-by-state basis. Furthermore, states define the license to drive as a privilege that they grant and revoke as they see fit.

For the most part, state-issued driver's licenses are already cross-referenced in a national database accessible to police and other agencies. Get stopped in New York for a traffic violation and present your Texas driver's license. It takes the New York police officer who stopped you no more than a few minutes to confirm the validity of your Texas license. But this is not enough for Big Brother.

In January 2002 the American Association of Motor Vehicle Administrators (AAMVA) proposed recommendations for establishment of a standardized driver's license and sharing of driver's license information between states and various agencies. Key among the AAMVA recommendations was: "Implement processes to produce a uniform, secure, and interoperable driver's license/ID card to uniquely identify an individual." A card to be shared between states and agencies, the express purpose of which is to "uniquely identify an individual," is a *national ID card*, regardless of what other "official" name it may be given!

This national ID card is being pushed in response to the September 11, 2001, terrorist attacks. There is, however, no evidence that a national ID card would have prevented the hijackings since the terrorists had government-issued visas, SSNs, and driver's licenses anyway. The AAMVA's proposal is unnecessary, oppressive, and would further destroy the rightful liberty of the American people. Today's "uniform, secure, and interoperable driver's license/ID card to uniquely identify an individual" is tomorrow's internal travel permit, permission to buy and sell, and license to receive health care or attend school. If you doubt this will happen, just consider what has happened with Social Security numbers!

As of October 1, 2000, federal law (42 U.S.C. Section 666(a)(13) makes it mandatory that you disclose your SSN to obtain any type of government license or recreational permit. This, of course, includes a driver's license and is just further evidence that the driver's license is nothing more than a national ID card by another name. We now have the Social Security number tied to the driver's license (and every other type of government-issued license). AAMVA would incorporate driver's licenses into an even more intrusive national database, subject to control, error, and abuse by government agencies.

States argue that the driver's license requirement does not restrict personal liberty (and courts have upheld this argument). They argue, "We are not restricting your freedom to travel, rather we are simply licensing the privilege of driving a motor vehicle. You can always use other modes of transportation." However, the last time I used another mode of transportation (flying aboard a commercial aircraft), the airline demanded to see my national ID card (err . . . driver's license) before allowing me to board the aircraft.

The claim that the common means of travel upon the public highways, travel by automobile, is a privilege to be licensed and controlled by Big Brother, effectively controls our personal liberty. You may, of course, walk where you will. There is no license required (yet) to travel by foot, but just how much personal liberty do you really have if the only way you can travel without Big Brother's written permission is to walk?

Because too many people accept this restriction on personal liberty and trade a constitutionally guaranteed freedom for a licensed and restricted privilege granted and taken away at Big Brother's whim, our freedom to travel is crushed under even greater restrictions and government oppression. Not only must we be licensed to exercise personal liberty, but we are also subjected to police roadblocks and checkpoints (often called "sobriety checkpoints")—bright lights, blocked roads, men with badges and guns, and a requirement that you submit to inspection all without probable cause (or even reasonable suspicion) that you have done anything wrong.

Strangely, the courts have upheld this shredding of the Constitution in the name of catching drunk drivers, holding that we give "implied consent" to these police checkpoints when we accept a driver's license. Yet every state makes it unlawful to exercise our personal liberty and travel upon the public highways by the common means of the day (automobile) without accepting a driver's license from the state! Catching drunks is no more justification for random police checkpoints than random searches of private homes to catch some other sort of criminal. No reasonable person would argue that the police should not be able to stop a vehicle whose the driver is obviously intoxicated or fleeing the scene of a crime. But the idea that Big Brother can set up a checkpoint, stopping American citizens at random and demanding "papers please," sounds suspiciously like the workings of a totalitarian police state.

So what can we do about the problem of having our personal liberty licensed and controlled by Big Bother? Driving without a driver's license is a misdemeanor in each state. If you are never stopped for an infraction of the various traffic regulations and are able to avoid Big Brother's random checkpoints, you could drive forever without ever possessing one of Big Brother's travel permits. Some may be willing to risk a misdemeanor charge and stand ready to argue personal liberty before the courts when necessary instead of submitting to Big Brother's licensing requirements. (It is interesting to note that if you are stopped without a driver's license but are in possession of other identification you may be charged with merely an infraction and not a misdemeanor.)

Some may choose to get a driver's license but arrange for the information input to Big Brother's database to be generally useless. While most departments of motor vehicles (DMV) will demand a street address for inclusion in their database, they will almost always be willing to send any correspondence to a "mailing address." A post office box need not be associated with your current physical address, and there is no one at the DMV running out to check the validity of street addresses on driver's license applications. Big Brother is demanding that SSNs be included on all driver's license applications, but I note that most states do not require any type of documentation confirming that number.

Some may simply choose not to drive a motor vehicle, thus never having a need to obtain a driver's license. This, of course, means giving up some degree of personal liberty to avoid becoming another number in Big Brother's ever-expanding databases.

Alternate ID may be used for just about anything where someone is demanding to see your driver's license for identification purposes. There is strong legal argument that licensing our personal liberty is abhorrent to the Constitution of the United States of America. Perhaps the time has come for us to tell Big Brother that we will no longer participate in his licensing games, nor will we any longer surrender our personal liberties for a government-granted privilege!

CHAPTER 46

Question Authority

Whenever confronted with a government regulation, policy, or agency requirement, the first question you should always ask is, "What gives you the authority to require me to do this (or prohibit me from doing that)?" Too often people assume that just because some government agency adopts and implements a policy that it actually has the authority to do so. Just because some bureaucrat states that something is a certain way does not mean that it is necessarily so. Let's take a look at a couple examples of assumptions people make with regard to government requirements.

Assumption #1: *With the constant demands that we provide our SSN for everything from filing taxes to getting a fishing license, there must be a requirement in the Social Security Act that all Americans get a Social Security number at birth, or at least prior to obtaining a paying job.*

Keeping the concept in mind that if the government requires me to do something it should have authority to make such a requirement, I wrote a letter to the Social Security Administration requesting that they show me where in the Social Security Act it states that a person is required to get a Social Security number. After all, the SSN has, for all practical purposes, become our national identification number.

About a month after I had written the letter, I received a response from the Social Security Administration signed by Charles H. Mullen, Associate Commissioner, Office of Public Inquiries. Mr. Mullen's letter stated, *"The Social Security Act does not require a person to have a Social Security Number (SSN) to live and work in the United States, nor does it require an SSN simply for the purpose of having one. However, if someone works without an SSN, we cannot properly credit the earning for the work performed."*

Mr. Mullen's letter went on to explain how the IRS uses the SSN as a taxpayer identification number and how one may not simply withdraw Social Security taxes already paid into the system. However, the leading part of his letter (and I believe the most important portion thereof) clearly states that the Social Security Act simply does not require that one have a SSN.

Assumption #2: *Speed limits are set by legal authority and are therefore indisputable matters of law. When a police officer issues a speeding citation, one may as well simply send in the payment since appearing in court to fight it is generally an exercise in futility.*

Many people have had the unpleasant experience of being stopped by a traffic cop for exceeding the posted speed limit (speeding). After being stopped, you surrender your driver's license, vehicle registration, and proof of insurance to the cop and wait while he runs all of this information through a computer system (either from a data terminal in his vehicle or by radioing the information in to a police dispatcher who runs the information on a station computer). Assuming that there are no major discrepancies between your papers and what's contained in the police database, you wait while the cop writes out a citation (traffic ticket). Now your papers will be returned along with the citation and a demand that you pay the associated fine (or appear in court). So many people just pay up when faced with this official version of highway robbery that many traffic tickets include envelopes within which to send in a payment.

However, the vast majority of speeding tickets are unfair, unjust, and written in violation of the government's own highway rules and regulations. The question to ask if you ever receive a speeding ticket isn't necessarily whether the cop had the authority to give you the ticket (although you should not overlook that possibility). Rather, you should inquire as to the authority by which the speed limit on the stretch of road where you were stopped was established in the first place. Many communities set arbitrary speed limits without the required engineering survey and then set up speed traps as a means of adding to the community's coffers. This abuse of authority involving traffic cops is so pervasive that the National Motorist Association (www.speedtrap.org) makes the following pledge to its members: "If, as a continuing member after one year of membership, you receive a speeding ticket and plead not guilty but lose in court, *NMA will pay your fine.*"

Because 90 percent or more of people presented with a traffic ticket simply pay it, unjust traffic citations continue to be used as a means of generating community revenue. However, the National Motorist Association points out that the majority of people who challenge these tickets and demand that the government prove its case will be found not guilty. After all, you can't be guilty of speeding if the posted speed limit itself isn't valid and was merely established at the whim of some bureaucrat. This is why the National Motorist Association can afford to pay your ticket if you lose . . . you probably won't!

However, the real point here is this: legitimate government in a constitutional republic derives its authority from the consent of the governed. We the People are a sovereign people, and we ought not surrender our rightful liberty to government agencies and to the public servants we elect and appoint to represent us.

When dealing with federal agencies, the provisions of the Freedom of Information Act (FOIA) give us the right to request that those agencies disclose information about their specific authority to do things. When dealing with state government agencies, we often have the same rights under the provisions of a state law that is similar to the federal FOIA. The FOIA and applicable state laws stipulate that government agencies are required to disclose to a requester any information that is not specifically held under listed exemptions (i.e., information classified for national security purposes).

Following is a sample letter that may be used to request information from federal agencies under the provisions of FOIA. The same basic format can also be used when requesting information from state agencies (though you will want to quote applicable state laws requiring its release).

Date

Your Name
Address
City, State, Zip

Agency Name

ATTN: FOIA Manager or Head of Agency
Address
City, State, Zip

Re: Freedom of Information Act Request

Dear Sir or Madam:

In accordance with the provisions of the Freedom of Information Act (5 U.S.C. Section 552, et al.) I request that you provide me with copies of the following records:

Item # 1
Item # 2, etc.

If there are any fees associated with researching or copying the requested information, please inform me of these fees prior to filling this request. The FOIA permits you to waive fees when the release of information is considered to be "primarily benefiting the public." I am requesting the above information for / to ____________ and believe this is clearly in the public interest. Therefore, I request that you waive any fees that may be associated with this request.

If any or all of my request is denied, I ask that you provide me with a copy of the specific exemption which you believe justifies the denial and inform me of appeals procedures available to me in this case.

I would be most grateful if you would handle this request as promptly as possible, and I look forward to your reply within 10 days as required by law.

Sincerely,

I have found that requiring government bureaucrats to disclose their authority for demanding this and that tends to keep those bureaucrats from running too far out of bounds. Often when one is faced with some kind of governmental bureaucratic nonsense, filing an FOIA request requiring disclosure of the government agency's specific authority to do what it is doing quickly clears up the problem. Even if the agency in question does have specific authority to do what it is doing, the FOIA request will aid you in clearly understanding the limits of that authority. FOIA and associated state laws are excellent tools for understanding the workings of our government and the limitations of governmental authority over us.

Chapter 47

Employ Countermeasures against Police Radar and Laser Detectors

Police radar and detectors to warn of its presence are good examples of the ongoing battle between Big Brother and American citizens who still value liberty. In 1973 the federal government mandated a "national speed limit" (55 MPH) and denied federal highway funds to any state that did not comply. The slower national speed limit was promoted as a "temporary" measure to conserve fuel; it had nothing to do with highway safety and was not initially promoted as such. However, as is usually the case with "temporary" or "limited" government restrictions, the claim that the 55 mph was a temporary measure for fuel economy turned out to be just one more government lie! Following the end of the fuel shortage concerns of the early 1970s, it became an almost constant political battle to get Big Brother to keep his promise that the national speed limit would be only temporary. It was not until 1995 that the national speed limit laws were finally scrapped . . . a 22-year temporary measure! It is also interesting to note that although the federal government denied highway funds to any state that did not comply with the national speed limit decree, no federal highway funds were set aside to help states absorb the cost of replacing speed limit signs, remarking no-passing zones, conducting engineering studies, and so on, following the final defeat of this "temporary" measure.

A general awareness that the national speed limit's promised temporary status had little meaning led to a majority of the population beginning to regularly exceed the 55 MPH limit. Local police agencies enforcing Big Brother's decree used radar to detect/confirm speed along our nation's highways, and an additional source of income began to flow into state coffers. (When given a traffic ticket, most people simply send in the money rather than contesting the ticket in court. You should never pay a traffic ticket without first challenging it in court!)

So with "Smokey" prowling the highways with radar and the American people being generally opposed to this intrusion into their liberty, we saw the development and expansion of a whole new market: radar detectors. After all, if government agents can track us with radar, we can use countermeasures to detect this surveillance.

Police radar operates in three bands: X-band (10.525 GHz), K-band (24.150 GHz) and Ka-band (34.7 GHz +/-). The X-band is no longer used exclusively by any state police agency and is generally being phased out in favor of K-band and Ka-band radar. X-band can still be found in use but suffers from interference problems caused by other things operating in the 10-GHz range. (In reviewing radar guns offered by the major manufacturers, I was unable to find an X-band radar offered as a current production model.)

Simply put, a radar detector looks for signals in these frequency ranges and sounds a warning when said signals are detected. To be effective, however, a radar detector must give you sufficient warning to allow you adjust your speed and thus avoid becoming another unwilling contributor to the state coffers by means of a traffic fine.

It is important to understand how radar is used in conjunction with traffic speed enforcement to understand how to employ countermeasures against it. The police officer conducting traffic speed enforcement (running a speed trap) will position himself where he can observe traffic (without being easily observed himself). The officer must now establish "visual tracking" of the vehicle he believes is speeding. He should be able to identify the vehicle by make, model (or body style), and color. He then confirms his opinion that the vehicle in question is exceeding the speed limit by activating his radar. The radar will only be triggered for a couple of seconds in order to get a lock on the vehicle in question. This is known as "Instant-On Radar." Now, if the vehicle the radar gets a lock on is yours, your radar detector will certainly let you know about it, but it will also be too late to do you much good.

A good radar detector should hear "Smokey" track someone else with radar and sound a warning before he has the chance to do the same to you. This concept works fairly well in that the police officer running the radar may simply use it on most vehicles as they come into range where they can be visually identified (about 1/4 mile). If you are traveling at 70 mph (102 feet per second) and your radar detector gives you warning of radar 1/2 mile ahead, you will have about 13 seconds to adjust your speed before coming into the 1/4-mile range where your vehicle can be visually identified. If, however, your detector is able to give warning at 1 1/2 miles from the radar, you will have about 65 seconds to adjust your speed before coming into the visual detection range of the police officer running the radar. It is important to be aware here that the 1/4-mile visual identification, while a reasonable estimate, is simply an example. Depending on terrain and amount of traffic, visual identification may be made at distances greater than 1/4 mile.

A trick used by police to fool radar detectors is to sit at the bottom of a hill and track vehicles with radar as they come over the crest of the hill. This initial radar lock can be made beyond reasonable visual identification range, requiring that the officer only keep the vehicle in sight until it comes close enough to be identified by make, model, color, and so on. The hill itself serves to block the radar signal, making it less detectable to radar detectors on the far side of the hill. The better-quality radar detectors will give some warning on the far side of a hill. In an urban area with lots of buildings, metal objects, and other vehicles to reflect the radar's signal, it isn't too difficult to make a detection from the far side of a hill; however, in open rural areas this becomes a much more difficult prospect.

So . . . just how accurate is police radar anyway? Under laboratory conditions it is very accurate; however, under field conditions police radar is subject to errors. In 1980 the National Bureau of Standards tested the top six police radar models. They found that all of the devices tested produced false speed-readings in the presence of police radio and CB radio. Furthermore, they found that all of the "moving radar" units were subject to shadowing, causing some of the patrol vehicle's speed to be added to the detected speed of the target vehicle (*Federal Register* 46:5, January 8, 1981).

The accuracy of police radar has certainly improved over the past 20 years; however, according to the National Bureau of Standards' Law Enforcement Standards Laboratory (LESL), the majority of errors in police radar are the result of environmental factors and operator error.

Yet even with the reports showing the error in police radar and the potential for environmental and operator error, the courts still tend to accept police statements about their radar readings as gospel. Because of this, it pays to be able to detect the presence of police radar when traveling along the nation's highways and byways.

Use of radar detectors is legal in all states except Virginia. Radar detectors are also illegal in Washington, D.C., and as of this writing, there is a bill in North Carolina that will make them illegal there if it passes.

So unless you live in Virginia or Washington, D.C. (and maybe North Carolina), it pays to install a radar detector in your personal vehicle. You will note that I specifically say "personal vehicle." This is because federal regulation makes it illegal to have a radar detector in any commercial vehicle: "No driver shall use a radar detector in a commercial motor vehicle, or operate a commercial motor vehicle that is equipped with or contains any radar detector."—49 CFR 392.71(a).

It should also be noted that radar detectors are illegal on all military installations: "The use of radar or laser detection devices to indicate the presence of speed recording instruments or to transmit simulated erroneous speeds is prohibited on DoD installations. Such devices shall not be sold in DoD-controlled sales outlets." —Department of Defense Instruction 6055.4, July 20, 1999, E3.11.3. Radar Detection Devices.

Radar detectors, like police radar itself, are subject to certain errors, but generally work well. If you do a lot of driving, a radar detector is certainly a worthwhile investment. Some manufacturers are adding additional features to their radar detector units, making them into highway information systems. In addition to the radar detection features, you can get electronic compasses, Global Positioning Systems (GPS), freeze alert to let you know when the roads may be icing up, strobe alert that detects approaching emergency vehicles, and many other options that you may find useful.

Although I like the idea of radar detectors, I am not a fan of laser detectors. The laser is a newer device being used in the ongoing effort to separate motorists from their money by way of traffic tickets. These lasers use a pulsed wave at 904 nanometers and emit a certain number of pulses per second. These pulses are reflected off the targeted vehicle and are used to determine the vehicle's speed. Unlike radar, which cannot pinpoint a specific vehicle in a group of vehicles, a laser can be targeted against a specific vehicle. In fact, it is specifically designed to target specific vehicles. The laser beam is only about 18 inches wide at 500 feet. All laser detectors will detect a laser pointed directly at them but will not generally detect a laser pointed at something else (like the car in front of you). Thus, they do not give you sufficient advanced warning as "Smokey" lights up other vehicles ahead of you. Once the laser is directed at your vehicle, the detector will give you warning, but by then it is too late to be of much value.

Some companies offer radar and laser jamming devices for use in your vehicle. Jamming a police radar requires the transmission of an active signal and is highly illegal. Fines for doing so range into the tens-of-thousands of dollars. Laser-defusing technology (i.e., as sold by K40 Electronics) would seem to offer some degree of defense against police laser but, as with laser detectors, requires that the laser actually target the defusing device to function effectively. Because laser for speed enforcement is a newer technology than radar, case law is less well defined with regard to the use of laser "jamming" devices.

Radar detectors and the associated technology are an excellent example of countermeasures technology in the battle between Big Brother and We the People. The majority of people driving our nation's highways do not support the currently established policy of speed limits and speed enforcement. If everyone (or even the vast majority) carefully complied with the arbitrary speed limits posted along our highways, there would be no need for police radar, radar detectors, lasers, and the ever-expanding technology of measures and countermeasures to protect us from "Smokey" and his speed traps as we travel along the public highways.

CHAPTER 48

Oppose the Use of Traffic Cameras

One of the greatest invasions of our privacy and assaults on our rightful liberties in the name of public safety is the use of cameras as a means of traffic enforcement. Many cities in the United States are installing cameras at intersections and along various highways. These cameras are linked to traffic signals at intersections and radar along the highways. Now, if you are going through the intersection when the light turns red, or traveling a bit over the speed limit, these cameras photograph your vehicle and a while later you receive a ticket in the mail with an order to pay the fine . . . or else!

Proponents of these traffic enforcement cameras claim that they cause drivers to slow down rather than attempt to rush through intersections at the last second, thus generally improving traffic safety while freeing police to focus on other, more important law enforcement matters.

Unfortunately, this just isn't true. Traffic cameras installed for the purpose of enforcing traffic regulations are simply another addition to Big Brother's surveillance society that serves as a cash cow for the municipality using them.

The city of Tempe, Arizona, conducted a study that showed that lengthening the yellow-light time at intersections would reduce red-light running as effectively as placing traffic cameras at these intersections. Nevertheless, recognizing the potential for adding to the city's coffers at the expense of its citizens, Tempe installed cameras at various intersections. The cameras were installed under contract with Lockheed Martin IMS. It is interesting to note that the contract prohibits the lengthening of yellow-light times at intersections where these cameras are being used.

House Majority Leader Dick Armey, in reviewing the use of cameras for traffic enforcement throughout the United States, has pointed out that some cities are actually shortening the yellow-light times at intersections. This results in a greater number of violations and thus a greater number of tickets being issued and fines being paid.

One June 27, 2001, British Columbia's Premier, Gordon Campbell, announced that he was putting an end to the province's 5-year traffic camera program. Campbell stated, "Speed cameras have no effect on road safety. They are nothing more than a cash cow. The Insurance Corporation of British Columbia (ICBC) funded the camera vans. Despite numerous studies, it could not prove that the photo-radar program had any direct effect on road safety."

However, the greatest condemnation of traffic enforcement cameras is not that they are ineffective or that they are simply a way for some municipality to add a few more dollars to the city coffers, or even that they are shortening yellow-light time (thereby creating a traffic hazard in order to cause more violations and gather a few more dollars). The greatest condemnation of these traffic cameras is that they completely disregard our constitutionally protected rights and freedoms in order to line Big Brother's pockets with a few more of our hard-earned dollars. Congressman Timothy Johnson (R-Illinois) has stated that traffic cameras are nothing more than a bounty system and are clearly unconstitutional. They violate our 14th Amendment guarantee of due process and equal protection under the law and our 4th Amendment protections against unreasonable search and seizure. Congressman Bob Barr (R-Georgia) has stated that these cameras eviscerate our constitutional guarantees against unreasonable search and seizure and the right to confront one's accuser.

But just how much money is involved here? How much money is enough for our government officials to trample our freedoms underfoot in the name of profit? The city of San Diego raked in about $7 million, with an additional $2 million going to contractor Lockheed Martin IMS. Yes, the contractor is receiving a kickback from revenue generated by its traffic cameras and the resulting fines. In San Diego, Lockheed Martin IMS received $70 from every $271 fine paid! In North Carolina the contractor received $35 from every $50 fine paid, and in that state camera tickets can't be appealed in court. There is an absolute presumption of guilt and a fine imposed without any provision for judicial review. In North Carolina if a thief steals your car and runs a red light making his getaway, you will receive a ticket in the mail and be expected to pay it!

If your city or state is using cameras for traffic enforcement it is important for everyone who has any regard for personal freedom and rightful liberty to oppose this practice in the strongest possible terms and at every possible opportunity. There are already proposals to further automate these systems to enable the government to automatically debit your bank account for any fines you may be assessed as a result of these cameras. After all, if, as in North Carolina, there is no provision for judicial review of these fines, why should Big Brother have to wait for you to send in the check if he can take the money from you immediately?

Surveillance technology, when used generally against American citizens, is a creeping pestilence that will certainly lead to the destruction of our freedoms and rightful liberties!

Chapter 49

Monitor Radio Traffic with a Scanner

Radio scanning is a fun and interesting hobby. Many "radio hobbyists" enjoy listening to radio traffic, monitoring police, fire, aircraft, and various public service frequencies. But, you might ask, what does this have to do with personal security and countermeasures?

Scanning your police, fire, and public service frequencies can give you advance notice of problems in your community. Hearing the police dispatcher send units to the local shopping center in response to a "man with a gun" would be a good indication to postpone your shopping trip. Hearing police report traffic stops can give you indication of where they are running their speed traps. Fire department and ambulance frequencies can indicate areas where emergency response vehicles are responding and allow one to avoid those areas and associated traffic slow-downs near any emergency response. Furthermore, in the case of area-wide disasters or other crises, monitoring public service frequencies gives you firsthand information from people on the scene. I have frequently obtained firsthand information from my radio scanners that alerted me to what was going on in my area long before there was any news report available.

As you get used to listening to the various official traffic coming across your scanner, you will learn to recognize the "problem areas" in your community. Get a street map of your area, and as you hear various radio traffic, plot the location of the incident on your map. After a few weeks (perhaps only several days) you will begin to see which areas are most prone to crime, where the local police are setting up their speed traps and checkpoints, and so on, and you will develop a better understanding of your community.

It should be noted that some areas have laws that prohibit using a scanner capable of monitoring "police frequencies" in your vehicle. Big Brother doesn't like the idea of citizens being able to monitor his activities and avoid his checkpoints. With this in mind, it should be noted that some of the states prohibiting mounting a scanner in your vehicle make an exception for anyone holding an amateur radio license. Florida, Indiana, Kentucky, Michigan, and Minnesota are examples. The FCC does not issue a "scanner license," and the amateur radio license is not required by the FCC to monitor amateur radio or other frequencies (only to transmit).

I recommend that anyone interested in personal security and countermeasures establish a private communications network. The most effective means of doing so is through amateur radio. The exception to the prohibition against scanners in vehicles for amateur radio operators is just one more reason to earn your amateur radio operator's license.

Chapter 50

Establish a Radio Network

Radios, while not providing very private communication, can provide effective communication when the normal communications infrastructure fails. Most people rely on the telephone system for communication. This may be landline telephones or cellular phones or both, but it is the same basic concept. If much of your communication is conducted via e-mail over the Internet, you may still be relying on the telephone system to allow you to dial up your Internet Service Provider. While e-mail is an excellent tool, it is just not the same as voice communication on the telephone.

With the ever-expanding cellular telephone technology, many people are relying on cellular telephones as their primary means of communication. Unfortunately, cellular telephones do not work everywhere. If there is no cell-site in range of your phone, the only thing you will get on your cellular telephone is a "No Service" or "Out of Range" message. Furthermore, during times of emergency, cellular networks can quickly become overloaded.

Even during time of peak usage (without any type of emergency), telephone circuits can become overloaded. Try to make a long-distance telephone call on Mother's Day or Christmas afternoon and you may find that the only thing you get connected with is a message saying, "All circuits are busy; please try your call again later."

Now, if getting overloaded once in a while was the only problem with telephone service, it would not be a matter for much concern. However, the biggest problem with telephone communication is that we do not control it. Whether your telephone call goes through or not is completely up to the whim of the phone company and the government!

Effective communication is essential for a free and sovereign people. Unfortunately, if you do not control the communications system your freedom to communicate is controlled by those who do. Although not highly publicized, the government and cellular telephone industry are working together to restrict access, by the general public, to cellular communications at the push of a button.

The December 12, 2001 edition of *The New York Times* contained an article entitled "U.S. Considers Restricting Cell Phone Use in Disasters." This article explained how, during times of "disaster," plans are to restrict cellular communication to government officials only. We certainly want emergency workers to be able to communicate effectively during an emergency, but do we want Big Brother to be able to shut down our ability to communicate with each other on a whim and with the flip of a switch? The government acknowledges that restricting public communication would pose a serious "inconvenience" to individuals trying to contact loved ones but argues that the needs of government take precedence over the needs of the people. Remember that today's minor inconvenience is tomorrow's major oppression as the web of government control continues to expand.

The most effective way to resolve the issue of control of our communications by Big Brother or some corporate bureaucracy is to control our own communications system. The easiest communications system for most of us to establish is a radio network.

This book isn't intended as a "radio" book; there are many such references available. However, I want to make you aware of the wide range of communications possibilities available in the United States of America.

Unlicensed Radio Services	**Licensed Radio Services**
Citizens Band (CB) Radio	Amateur (HAM) Radio
Family Radio Service (FRS)	Business Radio Service
Multi-use Radio Service (MURS)	General Mobile Radio Service (GMRS)
49 MHz Radios	Land Mobile Radio Service
	Maritime (Marine) Radio Service

Once you have radio equipment and have arranged a communication schedule with others, you may find that you depend less and less on the telephone company to contact friends and family. Of course, being able to communicate with someone via radio requires that both parties to the communication have a radio, but this is the intent of establishing an alternate communication system.

Depending on your personal requirements, you may be able to establish an alternate communications system with nothing more than a CB radio and a couple FRS handi-talkies. However, to establish a truly effective alternate communications system you will need to obtain an Amateur (HAM) Radio Operator's License. The requirements to obtain your license are minimal, the testing fee is just $10, and your license is good for 10 years.

A HAM radio station literally gives you the ability to communicate around the world. No longer are will you be dependent on Big Brother and corporate America to provide you with the ability to communicate. HAM radio offers all the advantages of shortwave listening with the major added benefit of being able to establish two-way communication when you want to.

Some of you may be thinking that you will just get yourself some HAM radio equipment and get on the air without bothering with getting the appropriate license. This is a very bad idea. **DO NOT ATTEMPT TO TRANSMIT ON AMATEUR (HAM) RADIO FREQUENCIES WITHOUT A VALID LICENSE AND CALL-SIGN!** HAM radio operators take a very dim view of anyone playing around on their frequencies without a proper license. One of the many aspects HAM radio is called "Fox Hunting," or, more accurately, radio direction finding. This means that if you start messing around on the amateur radio frequencies without a proper license you will be quickly located and will soon thereafter find Federal Communications Commission (FCC) agents knocking on your door to talk about your illegal activity and how many thousands of dollars in fines you now have to pay.

On the other hand, once you have your license and call-sign, you will be just one more call among thousands. You can be on the air when you want and talk with only those persons (stations) with whom you choose to talk. There are ways to maintain a degree of privacy in your HAM radio communications (and still remain 100 percent in compliance with the rules), so the fact that you have and use an FCC assigned call-sign is only a very minimal privacy problem. It would be a much greater privacy problem to try transmitting without a valid call-sign, just because of the amount of attention you would attract from every HAM operator who heard your illegal signals.

I am generally not a fan of government licensing and regulation, but the FCC (at least the Amateur Radio Section of the FCC) seems to be a fairly reasonable bunch. They assign your call-sign (after you have passed a very easy examination) and maintain the call-sign database. They coordinate frequency usage and generally leave the average HAM radio operator alone to enjoy his hobby—no inspections, reporting requirements, or annual fees. The only complaint (from a privacy standpoint) that one may have about the FCC Amateur Radio Section is that they consider your license data to be public information (it is available online at the FCC Web site). They publish your name, your license class, the date you were licensed, and your mailing address (you can use a P.O. box). I would like to see the FCC offer HAM radio operators the option of suppressing address information from public disclosure, but if you use a P.O. box as your license address (the FCC only requires a mailing address) this is a limited problem. Furthermore, throughout this book you will find various ways to keep your true location from being associated with your mailing address. The only thing most HAM radio operators ever receive from the FCC in the mail is a copy of their radio license. Once you have your license in hand, you won't have to worry about dealing with the FCC again for 10 years unless you upgrade or make changes to your license.

I have a HAM radio with me all the time. It allows me to stay in touch with friends around the world, to gather local information when I travel, and to have a personal communications system over which I have total control.

The ability to have 100-percent control over your personal communications equipment is a major asset to maintaining personal security. Although radio communication will not be the answer for everyone in every circumstance, it is certainly a good choice for many.

Chapter 51

Prepare for Emergencies and Disasters

Emergencies can occur at any time and in any place. They can range from a problem affecting a single individual or family to disasters affecting thousands of people and multiple states.

Prior to Y2K there were numerous books, articles, and videos produced about emergency preparedness, many of which provided excellent information that remains pertinent today.

From a personal-security point of view, it pays to heed the preparedness strategies written about in these books. If you are faced with some kind of emergency and have made no plans to deal with the situation, you will be forced to turn to government agents and agencies for whatever little assistance they may provide.

Most agencies (FEMA, Red Cross) that make recommendations about emergency preparedness suggest having 72 hours (3 days) worth of supplies on hand. Their rationale is that following any widespread emergency it will take about three days until the various relief efforts can be mobilized and brought up to speed.

For our purposes, however, it is necessary to have more than three days worth of supplies on hand. Having worked to develop a private, secure life, we will not be getting in line with every other "refugee" to be processed and provided for by any relief agency. I recommend that you maintain at least a two-week cache of supplies (more is better) to enable you to deal with any type of widespread emergency or disaster situation.

Your specific needs for a two-week period of total self-reliance will vary somewhat depending on where you live, but the basics remain fairly consistent. For those interested in personal preparedness, I strongly recommend two books as basic must-have references. The first of these is *Basic Preparedness* (The Survival Center, 1994). The second is *Aboman's Guide to Survival and Self-Reliance* by J.A. Bigley (aka Aboman). Aboman is also the owner/instructor of the Salmon Outdoor School in Tendoy, Idaho (www.aboman.com), where you can attend courses tailored to your specific needs to learn wilderness survival skills, primitive skills, and practical living skills. Finally, I highly recommend the award-winning Hoods Woods series of Woods Master and Cave Cooking videos produced by Ron and Karen Hood of Hoods Woods Wilderness Video Productions (P.O. Box 549, Garden Valley, ID 83622). One of the greatest resources offered by Hoods Woods is its free online survival forum and Web site at www.survival.com. The forum has 900+ members and a depth of experience and knowledge in survival and preparedness skills that is available nowhere else. In the survival forum you can correspond directly with such noted survival experts as Ron Hood, who has been teaching accredited wilderness survival courses for nearly 30 years; his wife and wilderness partner, Karen; J.A. Bigley; and desert survival skills wizard David Alloway, author of *Desert Survival Skills* (University of Texas Press 2000). You'll even find me on the forum from time to time.

Do your research and put together those basics, starting now. Don't let lack of preparedness destroy years of work in securing your personal privacy and rightful liberty. Don't become a refugee!

Chapter 52

Form a Mutual Support Group

No man, it has been said, is an island unto himself. We all have family and friends, people who share our interests and support our beliefs.

The 1990s saw the rise of the citizens' militias. These groups of like-minded people banded together to provide mutual support within the group, give aid to their communities, and, often enough, tell Big Brother to take a hike. Government favoritism of vocal minority groups at taxpayer expense, a growing disregard for our constitutional freedoms, and governmental atrocities at Ruby Ridge, Idaho, and Waco, Texas, fed the membership of these militias.

Today, many of these militias remain active in their communities. I strongly support the idea of a citizen's militia. However, the militia is not for everyone.

A similar concept that offers several advantages is the mutual support group. Here, a small group of individuals or families bands together for the mutual benefit of the group itself.

In his novel *Patriots: Surviving the Coming Collapse*, James Wesley, Rawles describes the structure of a mutual support group (survival group). While Rawles' book is a work of fiction, it makes very interesting reading for anyone interested in forming a mutual support group.

The advantages of being part of such a group are many. From a privacy and security standpoint, the group can serve to shield its individual members. For example, accounts can be established in the name of the group yet used by an individual member. In addition, groups have more buying power than individuals. I know of one small group of families in which each family was able to save an average of 25 percent of their monthly grocery bill simply by utilizing the group's increased buying power and taking advantage of bulk buying and sales. Furthermore, once the group is established it can actually provide better service to its members than can any government agency. The major advantage here is that the group becomes more and more self-reliant and less and less reliant on Big Brother. Simply put, when you are not part of the "system" you can not easily be affected by it.

It is important to remember that with a mutual support group the individual members work toward the benefit of the group yet still maintain their private and family lives. There should not be any type of forced commitment in a mutual support group, and every member must feel free to leave the group should he find that it is no longer suited to his needs. In this manner an individual or family can reap the benefits of a being part of a mutual support group without feeling trapped by it.

The following are some possible functions and advantages of a mutual support group:

home/co-op schooling
group buying power
mutual labor on group projects
varied skills and capabilities of members of the group (mechanic, doctor, plumber, paralegal, tailor, teacher, etc.)
mutual defense and protection (e.g., Neighborhood Watch)
mail receiving and forwarding
telephone forwarding
a support base for building individual sovereignty

Chapter 53

Don't Rely on 911

The advice most commonly given about how one should respond to a crime in progress is "dial 911." The idea is that as a crime begins to unfold you can reach a telephone, dial 911 (the emergency services number), and the police will rush to your aid, apprehend the bad guys, and save the day. While this is perhaps the ideal, in reality it seldom happens just that way.

We can divide the functions of the police into three broad categories: deterrence, investigation, and intervention.

Police deter crime through their presence. They conduct patrols and add a "police presence" to an area in order to reduce the level of crime. In their deterrence function the police tend to be very good. Criminals take great pains to ensure that they do not conduct their crimes in the presence of the police.

Once a crime has been committed the police will investigate in an attempt to determine what happened and who committed the crime. If they are able to determine the identity of the perpetrator the police will attempt to locate this person and arrest him. The effectiveness of the police investigative function varies greatly between police agencies and is highly dependent on the clues available at the crime scene. (Were there witnesses, fingerprints, or other forensic evidence?) Police tend to solve many crimes, but a large number of criminals get away with their crimes. The next time you are in a post office, look at the large number of "wanted" posters on the bulletin board. These criminals are all wanted for commission of a serious crime but haven't been caught (at least not yet).

The third major police function is intervention. The idea of intervention is that while a crime is in progress the police will arrive, stop the crime, and catch the criminals. This concept is the source of the commonly given advice of "dial 911 and wait for the police." It is here, however, that the police function is at its weakest. Police are seldom able to stop a crime in progress. The police simply can't be everywhere at once, and criminals make it a point to commit their crimes when the police are somewhere else. Even if you are able to call the police as a crime begins (or someone witnesses the crime and calls the police while it is in progress), the police may not be able to arrive in time to intervene. Finally, the police have no duty to protect any specific individual (with certain exceptions) from crime anyway. Most people believe that when they call 911 the police have a duty to respond as quickly as possible and render whatever assistance may be required. However, recognizing that the police simply cannot protect everyone, the courts have consistently ruled that police have no duty to protect any specific individual unless a special relationship exists between that individual and the police (i.e., the police may have a specific duty to protect the governor of their state).

One example of this can be seen in the case of *Warren v. District of Columbia* (D.C. Court of Appeals, 1981), in which three rape victims sued the city for failing to protect them from their attackers. In the early morning hours of March 16, 1975, three women were asleep in their home in northwest Washington, D.C. Two men broke through the back door of their home and entered the bedroom of the first victim, beating and sexually assaulting the woman in her own bed.

Hearing the struggle and the screams of their friend, the other two women, who had been asleep in an upstairs bedroom, called the police and told the dispatcher that someone was in their house and that they needed immediate help. Three police cruisers went to the women's address. One drove through the alley behind the home but apparently saw nothing amiss and did not stop. Officers also went to the front door and knocked but departed when they received no answer from inside.

Several minutes later, still hearing the screams of their friend below and still waiting for the police to come to their rescue, the two women hiding upstairs again called the police. The dispatcher assured the women that help was on the way and logged the call, but officers were never redispatched to the women's address.

After an hour had passed and the screams of their roommate had ceased, the two women went downstairs, assuming the police had arrived in response to their repeated calls for help. In fact, the police had not arrived; the initial victim's screams had stopped only because her attackers had beaten her into silence.

The words of the court describe in graphic detail what awaited the two women as they came downstairs: "For the next fourteen hours the women were held captive, raped, robbed, beaten, forced to commit sexual acts upon each other, and made to submit to the sexual demands of their attackers."

Having set out these facts, the court exonerated the District of Columbia, holding that police have no specific duty to protect individual citizens, no matter how urgent their call for help.

Although the Warren case dates from 1975, the concept that police have no duty to protect individual citizens still exists in Washington, D.C., today. Furthermore, the concept that the police have no duty to protect the individual citizen is not restricted to Washington D.C. This is a basic concept in the law of all of the 50 states.

The Warren case is not particularly unique or isolated, nor has the concept that the police have no duty to protect individual citizens changed over time. Consider the case of *Merced v. City of New York* (New York State Supreme Court, 1987).

Just after midnight on a warm summer night in June 1982, neighbors saw a man with a gun lurking near the New York City apartment of Mrs. Merced, a 22-year-old mother of one. The neighbors called 911 and waited for the police to arrive.

The police arrived a short time later and buzzed Mrs. Merced's apartment. Receiving no answer, they buzzed another apartment, and another tenant let them into the building. This tenant (not the one who had made the original 911 call), met the police in the hallway and told them that everything was OK. For whatever reason the police accepted this and never went to Mrs. Merced's apartment.

A short time later the neighbors who had originally called 911 called the police again, saying the police had not yet responded and help was still needed. The dispatcher radioed the officers who had been at the apartment building, but they reported that all was well and still did not go to Mrs. Merced's apartment.

The next day, neighbors went to Mrs. Merced's apartment, where they found her dead. She had bled to death from a gunshot wound.

Had the police actually gone to her apartment the previous evening, she may well have lived.

Mrs. Merced's estate brought suit against New York, claiming that the city was negligent in failing to respond after receiving the 911 call. After years of trail and appeal, the courts ruled that the estate could not recover any damages because Mrs. Merced had not personally called the police for assistance and therefore could not rely on any promise of assistance from them. Again, these laws are still in place.

There are numerous similar court cases, all involving the same basic scenario and all concluding with the same basic decision: the police have no specific duty to protect you!

Even though the police have no duty to protect you in most cases, many police officers will take great risks to protect the citizens of their states and residents of their communities. Police officers love to catch bad guys. Protecting the community, investigating crimes, and taking criminals off the street are the reasons most police officers join the police department in the first place. Unfortunately, the police cannot be everywhere at once, and even if they are present or are called to the scene of a crime they may not arrive in time to intervene and protect you from becoming the victim of a violent criminal attack. Police policy, procedure, and politics can create a set of circumstances wherein investigations are incomplete or indicators of pending violent crimes are overlooked.

Take the case cited by Special Agent Daniel Schofield's article in the *FBI Law Enforcement Bulletin* (January 1991), "When Do Police Have a Constitutional Duty to Protect?" Michael and Deborah had been in a relationship for many years. In fact, Deborah was the mother of Michael's two children. This was not, however, an easy relationship. In 1989, Deborah had filed a battery charge against Michael but had later withdrawn it. The threat of criminal prosecution did little to restrain Michael's violent temper, and over the next few years things became progressively worse.

During the first half of 1994, Deborah's mother called the police at least six times to report that Michael had abused Deborah.

On June 21, 1994, Deborah called the police to report Michael's abuse, expressing her fear that Michael would further harm her and their two children. The police responded and helped Deborah and her children move out of the family home.

At the same time, Deborah obtained a temporary protective order from the court ordering Michael not to contact, harass, or abuse her. While she was waiting for the police to serve him with the protective order, Michael located her and took her car. Deborah called the police and told them that Michael had taken her car and was in violation of the temporary protective order. Even though two days had passed since the court had issued the order, the police had not yet served Michael with the order, and until he had been served with the order he could not be arrested for violating it.

Three days later Michael went to the house where Deborah was staying with their children, broke a window, entered the house, hit Deborah in the head with a pistol, choked her, and threatened to come back and kill her.

Following a 911 call by Deborah's mother to report the attack on her daughter, the police located and arrested Michael. At that point they served him with the temporary protective order issued by the court back on June 21. They also took him to jail for his attack on Deborah. At arraignment the court set Michael's bail at $75,000 and released him, ordering him to comply with the temporary protective order and stay away from Deborah.

Within a week, Deborah again called the police to report that Michael was threatening her and the children. Michael was arrested the same day, but despite his violation of the court's temporary protective order and the other charges against him, he was released on an additional $500 bond.

Believing Michael to be in jail, Deborah and her children moved back to their home, which they had fled back to on June 21. Deborah was accompanied by her brother Scott and friend James. At about 1:40 P.M., Deborah again called 911, reporting that Michael had broken into the house and requesting immediate help.

The police raced to the scene, arriving in just a few minutes. Unfortunately, it was a few minutes too late. The police found Deborah, Scott, and James all murdered by Michael, who had then killed himself.

The police had responded to the 911 call, but for Deborah, Scott, James, and the family members they left behind, help had come too late.

You must be prepared to protect yourself from crime, to defend your person and property from attack. If your only plan is to "dial 911," you may "dial 911 and die!"

Chapter 54

Improve Your Personal Protection Skills

The choice of whether to own a firearm for personal protection is one that should be left entirely up to the individual. Although various oppressive government agencies and antifreedom organizations constantly work to infringe on our constitutional freedom to keep and bear arms, that freedom is one that we must never surrender.

For those of us who choose to keep and bear firearms for personal protection, it is incumbent upon us to learn to use those firearms competently. No matter what you may think of the National Rifle Association (NRA) with regard to its political activities in defense of the Second Amendment, you cannot dispute that it provides good basic firearms and safety instruction. The NRA Personal Protection Course provides training in the fundamentals needed to use a firearm for personal protection. There are certainly more in-depth courses from big-name shooting schools, but not everyone is in a position to attend those schools. The courses themselves tend to be expensive, and attending the school will likely require some travel.

The NRA Personal Protection Course is taught throughout the country by local firearms experts who have completed an NRA certification program. The cost of the course is generally less than $100, making it affordable for most anyone in a position to carry a firearm for personal protection.

In addition to its Personal Protection Course, which is focused on using a firearm for personal protection, the NRA offers a program called Refuse to Be a Victim (RTBAV). The RTBAV course focuses on other methods of personal protection, emphasizing awareness and crime prevention techniques. Realizing that not everyone will choose to use a firearm for personal protection, the NRA designed the RTBAV course to provide training in alternative methods of personal protection. The RTBAV course is generally offered for just a few dollars and is available throughout the country.

Both of these NRA courses provide people with skills that enable them to protect themselves from criminal attack. We have already seen that dialing 911 may not be the best option when faced with a criminal attack. Therefore, your mind-set should always be that you will resolve our own problems and, if necessary, let local officials complete the necessary paperwork afterwards.

So whether you choose to keep a firearm for personal protection or not, there are low-cost courses available through the NRA that will improve your overall personal protection skills. For more information on either of these programs, visit the NRA Web site at www.nra.org.

CHAPTER 55

Legally Resist Firearms Registration

The right of the people to keep and bear arms is one of the most significant individual freedoms guaranteed to American citizens and enumerated in the U.S. Constitution. It is also the freedom most often attacked by rogue government agencies and the haters of freedom.

When you go to your local sporting goods store to purchase a rifle, shotgun, or pistol, you will be required to fill out various forms, present identification, and await the results of a background check before you can take possession of the firearm you are buying. In some of the more oppressive areas of the country, you will also be required to further register your firearms, obtaining licenses and permits in order to exercise your constitutionally protected freedom to keep and bear arms.

This registration of firearms and, by default, of the owners of said firearms is an intolerable infringement on the rightful liberty of American citizens. It is a well-established principle of law that "where rights secured by the Constitution are involved, there can be no rule making or legislation which would abrogate them." (*Miranda v. Arizona,* 384 U.S. 436, 468). Yet where the Second Amendment is concerned those rights are daily trampled underfoot.

Lists of firearms and their owners almost always lead to confiscation of these firearms as governments become more oppressive. We have recently seen this to be true in Great Britain and Australia. We have even seen it in some areas of the United States. In 1967, New York City passed an ordinance requiring one to obtain a permit to purchase a rifle or shotgun. These firearms were thus registered with the city. Concerns that the lists of registered firearms owners would be used at some future date to confiscate or ban firearms ownership were dismissed as right-wing paranoia. "We are just trying to keep guns out of the hands of criminals," cried city officials. "Honest firearms owners have nothing to fear." In 1991, New York City passed a ban on the private ownership of semiautomatic rifles and shotguns. The registration lists were used to inform New York City residents that they must take their firearms out of the city, destroy them, or surrender them to the police.

The same type of firearms confiscation took place in California tin 1998 when former Attorney General Dan Lungren ordered residents to turn in their SKS rifles. Just which California residents were required to surrender their firearms? That's right—only those law-abiding citizens who had complied with California's firearms registration requirements!

It is interesting to note that convicted felons cannot be required to register their firearms! In *Haynes v. US* (309 U.S. 85, 1968), the U.S. Supreme Court ruled that since felons are prohibited from owning firearms to begin with, a regulation requiring firearms to be registered may not be applied to a convicted felon as such a requirement would violate his rights against self-incrimination under the 5th Amendment. Thus, the only people who can be required to register firearms are honest, law-abiding men and women, and when those registration lists are used to compel us to surrender our firearms, it will only be honest men and women who will be deprived of their firearms. Criminals will still have their firearms because they are not on Big Brother's list of firearms owners!

While there may be something to be said for civil disobedience bringing about political change, I do not recommend that anyone act in violation of the established law. However, there is a perfectly legal way in which one may obtain firearms without ending up on some government list to be used in future confiscation. Buy firearms through private sale and trade firearms with other owners and collectors.

There is nothing (yet) that prevents honest men and women from buying and selling their own property and trading that property with one another. If you purchase a rifle from someone at your local hunting club, there is no government-held record of that transaction; thus, Big Brother does not know you own that rifle. If you and a friend each have a handgun that the other wants and you can agree on a trade, you will each have a pistol that Big Brother won't have a record of when planning the next round of firearms confiscation.

The intent here is not to establish some underground firearms business but rather to exercise our constitutional freedoms as free and honest sovereign citizens without ending up on another of Big Brother's lists.

Chapter 56

Get the Other Side of the Story

Are you tired of the mainstream media's politically correct sound-bite reporting? Have you ever wanted to hear the other side of the story? There are a number of alternate media sources available that provide unique insights into current affairs and government activities.

These alternate publications tend to be strongly supportive of our rightful liberty and constitutional freedoms. Because of the nature of their reporting, they tend to identify threats to our rightful liberty and often offer countermeasures to these threats. By using these alternate sources, you will find information that would never be reported by the mainstream media.

Certainly continue to watch your local news reports and international news from sources like CNN, but don't forget that there may be more to the story than you are hearing on the eleven 'o clock news. Subscribe to one or more of the following alternate news sources (or some other alternate news source that you find reliable) and get a more complete perspective on the goings on in the world:

Free American—Clay Douglas' excellent monthly magazine, *Free American* (www.freeamerican.com) offers articles, features, and resources seldom heard in the mainstream media.

Jubilee Newspaper—A quarterly "Newspaper of Record for the American Christian Patriot." If you want the "other side of the news" from a fundamental Christian perspective, *Jubilee Newspaper* (www.jubilee-newspaper.com) will certainly be of interest.

Media Bypass—*Media Bypass*: The Uncensored National News (www.mediabypass.com) is another monthly news magazine providing relevant news and investigative reporting of events not covered by the mainstream media.

The New American—The magazine of the John Birch Society. *The New American* (www.thenewamerican.com) provides strongly conservative reporting of government activity. Strongly supports U.S. Constitutional Freedoms.

Sierra Times —*Sierra Times* (www.sierratimes.com) bills itself as "An Internet Publication for Real Americans." This is an excellent online resource for "The Other Side of the News," offering both a free area and a subscribers/members-only area.

World Net Daily—"A Free Press for a Free People," *World Net Daily* (www.worldnetdaily.com) is an online news resource.

No source listed here should be taken as a sole, definitive news resource. Yet, as I stated earlier, in order to counter threats to our rightful liberty we must be aware that those threats exist. Alternate media sources can give you that early warning not found in the mainstream press.

CONCLUSION

Aspire to Sovereignty

Focusing on the ever-increasing intrusion into our private lives by Big Brother, corporate bureaucracies, and various criminals, this book has presented many suggestions for enhancing privacy and personal security.

As you become more and more aware of the threats to your privacy and personal security and begin to employ countermeasures to those threats, you will find yourself becoming more and more self-reliant and independent.

It is important to remember that We the People are a sovereign people and that we must not surrender our rights and freedoms to government agencies and the public servants that we elect and appoint to office. Too often our public servants think that once they are in office they become the public's masters, but we do not need to play their game or tolerate their attacks on our rightful liberty. We need only declare our independence, one by one, from the malignant culture that poisons our very lifeblood as a people.

There is a quietly growing movement of sovereign citizens who have declared their independence from Big Brother and choose to no longer be part of a corrupt and malignant system. These people see the downward spiral of eroding freedom and lost rightful liberty that is being allowed in the name of "political correctness" and "government control," and they have chosen to reclaim their liberty and freedom.

Some may ask whether there is really any need to be concerned with the current trends in government. After all, although current government policies may cause some inconvenience from time to time, most of us "have nothing to hide" and can put up with "a little tightening of our freedoms" in the name of increased safety. In response to this I again stress that today's minor inconvenience is tomorrow's oppression:

> When Hitler came for the Jews . . . I was not a Jew, therefore, I was not concerned. And when Hitler attacked the Catholics, I was not a Catholic, and therefore, I was not concerned. And when Hitler attacked the unions and the industrialists, I was not a member of the unions and I was not concerned. Then, Hitler attacked me and the Protestant church — and there was nobody left to be concerned.
>
> —Pastor Martin Niemoller, *Congressional Record* October 14, 1968, vol. 114, p. 31636

As Benjamin Franklin pointed out in the early days of this great republic, "Those who would give up essential liberty to purchase a little temporary safety deserve neither liberty nor safety." We must never surrender our rights and freedoms, no matter how just and well meaning the cause may seem at the time.

There is much to be said in favor of the "sovereign citizen" movement. Unfortunately there are also those who in the name of individual sovereignty are little more than criminals and con men. Be very, very cautious of any group or individual wanting to charge you hundreds or thousands of dollars to help you reclaim your individual sovereignty. This is almost always a scam or, at best, highly overpriced information that is readily available for free to anyone willing to invest the time and effort in research.

We can look at an excellent example of sovereignty at work among the Amish. The Amish are a very conservative group of Christians who lead their lives simply and avoid much government and bureaucratic intrusion into their lives by simply refusing to participate. I am not personally ready to go join an Amish order, although there is some appeal to the idea. However, there is much that one seeking individual freedom and sovereignty can learn from the way the Amish hold themselves separate from today's corrupt and malignant system.

A group of people having a sincere belief that they should hold themselves apart from the "ways of the world" might be able to achieve significant amounts of privacy and freedom simply by no longer participating in government bureaucracy.

In addition to choosing not to participate in the "system," many sovereign citizens involve themselves in the study of common law, constitutional history, and the proper function of government. Some of their legal and historical research can be very complex, yet it often leads to greater understanding of and desire to protect our rightful liberties.

For those willing to devote the time and research, sovereign citizenship may be the ultimate countermeasure against Big Brother and corrupt bureaucracy.

APPENDIX I

Web Sites for Freeware Downloads

Counterpane Labs (Password Safe)
www.counterpane.com/labs.html

Password Gates (and Other Web Site Tools)
www.bravenet.com
www.4allfree.com
www.cgiforme.com
http://sethweb.frogspace.net/Simply_Secure/index.html
www.hits4me.com
www.sitegadgets.com
www.authpro.com

Pretty Good Privacy (PGP)
http://web.mit.edu/network/pgp.html

ScramDisk
www.scramdisk.clara.net

ZipLip E-mail
www.ziplip.com

Appendix II

Retailer and Resource Addresses

Caveat Emptor—Buyer Beware: Although I believe all companies listed below to be reputable, I can make no guarantees that their products and services will meet your needs. Please conduct your own investigation to determine the suitability of any company before conducting business with it.

CASH CARDS INTERNATIONAL, LTD.
Armory Building, Victoria Road
Basseterre, St. Kitts, West Indies
Fax: 869-466-7355
Web site: www.cashcards.net

COMMUNICATIONS SYSTEMS-EAST
1 Federal Street
Camden, NJ 08103
Web site: http://www.L-3com.com/privatel/

ELECTRONIC FRONTIER FOUNDATION
454 Shotwell Street
San Francisco, CA 94110-1914 USA
Fax: 415-436-9993
Web site: www.eff.org

F-SECURE CORPORATION
Tammasaarenkatu 7
PL 24
00180, Helsinki Finland
Fax +358 9 2520 5001
Web site: www.europe.f-secure.com/index.shtml

KEYKATCH
Daniel Wegner, Inc.
15510 Territorial Road
Maple Grove, MN 55369
Web site: www.keykatch.com

MURRAY ASSOCIATES
P.O. Box 668
Oldwick, NJ 08858-0668
Web site: www.spybusters.com

NATIONAL MOTORISTS ASSOCIATION
402 West 2nd Street
Waunakee, WI 53597
Web site: www.speedtrap.org

POSTAL WATCH, INC.
3631 Virginia Beach Blvd., # 100
Virginia Beach, VA 23452
E-Mail: info@postalwatch.org
Web site: www.postalwatch.org

SHOMER-TEC
Box 28070
Bellingham, WA 98228
Web site: www.shomer-tec.com

SPECTORSOFT CORPORATION
333 17th Street
Vero Beach, FL 32960
Web site: www.spectorsoft.com

TRANSCRYPT SECURE TECHNOLOGIES
4800 NW 1st Street, Suite 100
Lincoln, NE 68521
Web site: www.transcryptsecure.com

Appendix III

Security Checklist

- ❑ Call opt-out number to prevent credit reporting agencies from selling your credit information.

- ❑ Send letters to your financial institutions instructing them not to disclose information about you in accordance with the Gramm-Leach-Bliley Act and the Fair Credit Reporting Act.

- ❑ Contact the Direct Marketing Association and opt out of direct mail and telephone marketing services.

- ❑ Send letters to each of the major companies engaged in direct marketing and require that your name and address be removed from their marketing lists.

- ❑ Contact each of your financial institutions, credit card companies, and service companies where you have accounts and establish a telephone password for these accounts.
- ❑ Download, install, and use PGP for your e-mail.
- ❑ Install a BIOS password on all your computers.
- ❑ Purchase a paper shredder and shred all documents before throwing them in the trash.
- ❑ If you use a cordless telephone, be sure that it operates in the 2.4 GHz range and employs spread spectrum technology.
- ❑ Don't subscribe to things under your own name . . . use an alias.
- ❑ Establish an alternate identity to protect your personal privacy.
- ❑ Consider the advantages of a mutual support group in protecting your privacy.

Bibliography and Selected Reading

Charrett, Sheldon. *Identity, Privacy, and Personal Freedom*. Boulder: Paladin Press, 1999.

Lunna, J.J. *How to Be Invisible*. New York: St. Martin's Press, 2000.

Mandia, Kevin, and Chris Prosise. *Incident Response: Investigating Computer Crime*, Berkeley: Osborne/McGraw-Hill, 2001.

Rawles, James Wesley. *Patriots: Surviving the Coming Collapse*. Lafayett, LA: Huntington House Publishers, 1999.

Sweeney, H. Michael. *The Professional Paranoid*. Los Angeles: Feral House, 1998.

Wolfe, Claire. *Don't Shoot the Bastards (Yet)*. Port Townsend, WA: Loompanics Unlimited, 1999.

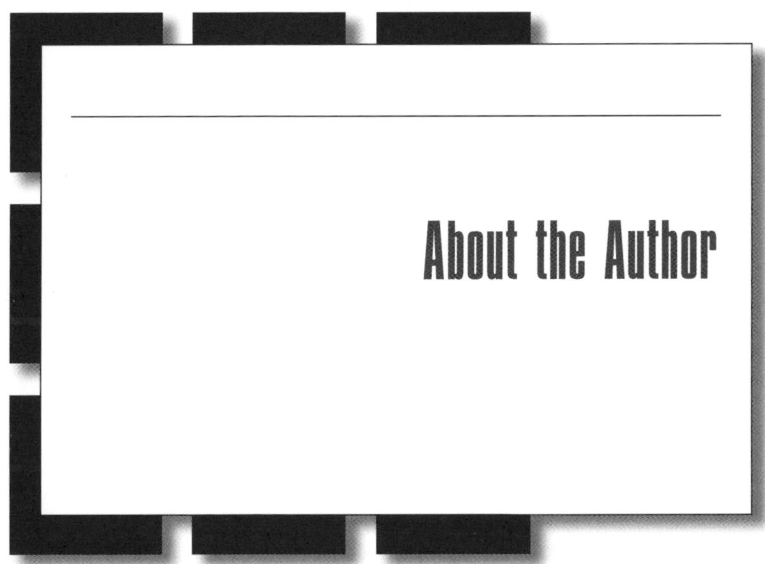

About the Author

Michael Chesbro retired as a senior counterintelligence agent from U.S. Department of Defense Special Operations after more than 21 years of service. He holds degrees in security management, paralegal studies, and jurisprudence and is a graduate of the Federal Law Enforcement Training Center. He is professionally certified as a protection officer and security supervisor by the International Foundation for Protection Officers. He is a board-certified forensic examiner and fellow of the American College of Forensic Examiners, as well as a diplomate of the American Board of Forensic Examiners and the American Board of Law Enforcement Experts.

Since his retirement from government service, Michael Chesbro devotes his time to writing, technical research, and consulting and serves as the director of the Auroral Radio Research Group (Radio Reconnaissance).